MW00998747

UNDERCURRENT

UNDERCURRENT

Tank Commander Cadet in the Yom Kippur War

AMIR BEGA

CASEMATE

Philadelphia & Oxford

Published in the United States of America and Great Britain in 2023 by
CASEMATE PUBLISHERS
1950 Lawrence Road, Havertown, PA 19083, USA
and
The Old Music Hall, 106–108 Cowley Road, Oxford OX4 1JE, UK

Hardcover Edition: ISBN 978-1-63624-341-2
Digital Edition: ISBN 978-1-63624-342-9

A CIP record for this book is available from the British Library

Printed and bound in the United Kingdom by CPI Group (UK) Ltd, Croydon, CR0 4YY
Typeset in India by DiTech Publishing Services

For a complete list of Casemate titles, please contact:

CASEMATE PUBLISHERS (US)
Telephone (610) 853-9131
Fax (610) 853-9146
Email: casemate@casematepublishers.com
www.casematepublishers.com

CASEMATE PUBLISHERS (UK)
Telephone (0)1226 734350
Email: casemate-uk@casematepublishers.co.uk
www.casematepublishers.co.uk

Front cover image: Author's personal collection

In Memory of Shabtai and Yoav

Contents

Glossary

8×30 binoculars:	Type of binoculars used by the Armor Corps.
American Patton:	A type of tank (Patton M48) that was in use by Israel Defence Forces.
Anti-tank Sabot shell:	Main tank ammunition (see APDS).
APC:	An Armored Personnel Carrier is a military vehicle designated to transport personnel and equipment in combat zones.
APDS:	Armor Piercing Discarding Sabot; Main gun tank ammunition designed to destroy an armored fighting vehicle.
Beretta 9 mm:	Semi-auto pistol Beretta M9.
Browning 0.3:	M1919 Browning is a 0.3 caliber medium machine gun used during the 20th century.
Co-axial machine gun:	Machine gun mounted parallel to the tank cannon; This allows the machine gun to aim using the cannon gun control.
Halon fire extinguisher:	Electrically non-conducting fire extinguisher. It is ideal for armored vehicles and spacecraft because it produces less toxicity.
HEAT:	High Explosive Anti-Tank. Tank ammunition designed to destroy an armored fighting vehicle, APC, and infantry.
HESH rounds:	High Explosive Squash Head. Tank ammunition designed to destroy an armored fighting vehicle, APC, and infantry.

Hull-down position:	Battle tank position—The main body (Hull) is behind a crest or other raised ground protected from enemy fire, but the turret is exposed and able to fire.
Kfir Jets:	Israeli-manufactured combat aircraft.
Kibbutzim:	Israeli collective community settlements (Plural).
Long-Tom cannons:	M1 155mm heavy field gun (artillery) developed and used by the US military.
M3 half-track:	An armored personnel carrier half-track.
MG:	Machine gun.
MiG:	A Russian/Soviet military fighter aircraft.
Nomex:	A synthetic fabric having heat and flame resistance.
Reo crane trucks:	Military mobile crane.
RPG:	Rocket Propelled Grenade—Shoulder-fired missile.
RPM:	Revolutions Per Minute—number of turns an engine crankshaft makes a full rotation in a minute.
Sagger:	Anti-Tank-wired-guided missile system (Malyutka).
Shot-Kal tank:	An upgraded version of the famous WWII British Centurion.
Tiran tank:	An Israeli upgrade version of the Russian tanks T-54 & T-55 captured from Egypt and Syria during the Six-Day War in 1967.
Tracer bullet:	Bullets with a small pyrotechnic charge in their base; when fired, it's ignited, making the projectile visible.
Turret-down position:	Full cover position—The main tank body (Hull) and the turret are behind a crest or other raised ground protected from enemy fire.
Uzi:	Israeli-made submachine gun.

Prologue

Toronto, Summer 2019

It's a death trap!

Time to jump. No, not yet. I should hold on a little longer. I'm still too high up and too far away. Wait! Wait! This isn't good enough.

Thoughts race through my mind. *I must jump now. Otherwise, I will die. I can't wait any longer.*

It's time. I drop my heavy military gear and my Uzi gun on top of the turret where I usually sit. Everything else is in the loader cell inside the turret. There's no time to grab my personal belongings. It's too late for that.

The ferry tilts to its left, and the tank is on a steep sideways angle. *Oh, God, it can't hold its position!* I can hear the tank's metal claws screeching against the ferry's steel floor as it begins to slide sideward. The tank gains speed, sliding toward the metal railing at the ferry's edge and hitting it.

With a thud, the iron monster begins to tip over.

I can hear our gunner, Yoav, who sits below our commander, Shabtai, screaming:

"Let me out! Help me!

Get out! You're blocking my way out.

Let me out!"

I glance to my right and see Shabtai. *Why is he ducking down inside the turret? By now, he should be on top of the turret, ready to jump as he has ordered us to, leaving a chance for Yoav to escape after him. And yet he's going back inside, into the capsizing tank. Why?*

I pull the helmet from my head and drop it down on the turret. *Now I have no way of communicating with my crew. I am on my own.*

I must focus on the jump.

My life depends on this jump.

Timing is crucial. Jump too early, and I will crash onto the ferry's metal floor. Too late, and the tank will flip over me and pull my body down to the bottom of the Suez Canal.

I need the angle of the tilt to be 45 degrees to maximize my distance from the tank. I must be as far away as possible when the tank and the ferry hit the water. I try to estimate the angle. *Forty degrees, maybe? I need to wait. Another breath. Another moment.*

Now!

Now!

I strain every muscle in my body to the extreme. Using all my strength, I push myself up with my legs from my squatting position on top of the turret, to flinging myself into the air.

Oily, smelly water rushes over me. It's so quiet in the dark depths that momentarily, I'm deaf and blind. Completely alone. The water vortex caused by the plummeting tank drags me down to the bottom of the Suez Canal and blocks my feeble attempts to swim up to the surface. I can't breathe. I can't see. I can't hear.

How long can I survive without breathing?

How long can I stay awake?

I want to breathe, I need air, or I will die in the water.

No. I can't give up.

Air! Air! My body screams for air.

★★★

I gasp and wake up, confused, breathing heavily. My heart pounds in my chest, and my body is damp with sweat. My wife lies in bed next to me, still asleep. I have not woken her up. My miniature schnoodle is stirred awake by my sudden movement, rolls onto his back, and demands belly scratches.

The early morning light is seeping in from behind the drapes in my bedroom, and as my heartbeat slows down, I hear sounds of the morning outside. Birds are tweeting, cars are driving around the neighborhood, and a bus stops at the corner of the street, announcing "Autumn Boulevard" to the passengers getting off. This quiet suburb I call home is awakening to a new day.

Relax. Control yourself.

I have had this nightmare many times before, but I'm okay, healthy, and safe. *Am I?*

How can it be? Almost 50 years have passed, yet these images have stayed with me, etched clearly in my mind's eye as if the war had happened only yesterday.

CHAPTER I

Shivta, Israel, October 5, 1973

Armored Corps—The Tank Commanders' Academy

Israel—50 km south of Be'er-Sheva

The four-month period of intensive training for tank commanders, consisting of 20 working hours a day, had just ended. All the cadets were exhausted.

As part of the curriculum, we had been divided into crews of four cadets each, and assigned a tank. During training, each team was entirely responsible for its tank. We learned how to operate the tank in every role—as commander, driver, loader, and gunner. We practiced tactical movements and military strategies, gained experience in using all weapon systems, and exercised standard orders and commands.

As tank commanders, we were responsible for guiding our crewmen in operating the machine in all its functions, from driving directions to using weapon systems and problem-solving.

As drivers, we learned how to skillfully maneuver through different terrains, act in emergency situations, and maintain the powertrain.

As loaders, we were responsible for maintaining the weapon systems and loading the main guns and machine guns. We also took care of radio communications—external and internal. And standing in our hatches next to the commander, we served as his second pair of eyes.

As gunners, we were trained to use all kinds of guns, shoot targets, and watch for enemy threats using the periscope. Gunner cells were below the commander's hatch.

The tanks were maintained constantly and kept tidy. It was an essential requirement that they be fully operational and ready for action at all times.

There was one final inspection to pass before leaving the base for a long weekend, a vacation, and we were all eager to go. It was Yom Kippur, the Day of Atonement, that Saturday.

The tank had to be in pristine condition, from top to bottom, to get through the inspection. We started with the weekly maintenance. Lubricating and cleaning the cannons and the

The author standing on top of a *Shot-Kal.*

machine guns, greasing the wheels, checking the engine and transmission, and dusting the air filters, toolsets, and tank equipment.

We cleaned our tanks all night long. Ours was spotless by the time we finished—a shiny white on the inside and beige-green on the outside. We tightened the tracks to their proper tension and replaced any missing or damaged parts. Then, we organized all working tools and spare parts into internal and external storage bins and covered the turret with a square canvas. Covering the tank was essential. The heavy steel tracks of our beasts ground the sandy terrain underneath them into fine particles. Combine that with a blowing wind carrying powder-like dust, and our cleaning efforts could be ruined in a moment.

Finally, we were ready for inspection.

Our instructor came at first light, climbed up on the tank, opened his checking list, and checked it off item by item. Everything was completed to his satisfaction, from inside to out.

"Good job. Everything is fine. Just brush an additional layer of oil inside the cannon barrel and close the lids back down," he said.

I was happy. I climbed on the turret and closed the loader, commander, and driver hatches. Meanwhile, my two crew members poured oil on a brush and applied it to the cannon barrel.

★★★

Dawn broke over the horizon. We walked toward our barracks on the north side of the base through a pathway covered with asphalt, made of black tar and sand, and marked by white stones on both sides.

The long line of small, single, ground floor rooms, with a long corridor, reminded me of a youth hostel I had lodged in as a boy scout.

It was time to prepare for the final inspection of our rooms, personal equipment, and attire. Outside, the temperature was climbing fast; the desert region's fierce sun had no mercy on us, and in a short time, the rooms were sweltering. And in that already scorching morning heat, we worked quickly to organize our rooms. Each room accommodated eight cadets on four bunk beds that stood head-to-toe alongside two walls. The window was on the north side wall, across from the door that opened to the corridor.

Before making the beds, we helped each other shake the dust off the three wool blankets on each bed. Then, one blanket was straightened and tightened on the mattress, and the other two folded neatly on the end of the bed. The bedding was so tight and crisp that you could easily have bounced a quarter off it. On top of the blankets, in perfect alignment, we placed two square, fully equipped military backpacks—a haversack and a rucksack—combat webbing equipment, and a sleeping bag. And on the floor next to the bed lay a large army kitbag containing our personal belongings.

Next, we cleaned our personal guns—the Uzis. And lastly, we washed the floor with a bucket of water and towels, and removed the sandy dust from corners and windows.

Finally, our household chores were done. Our mothers would have probably approved, but we needed our commanders to okay our work.

I ran to the shower hut on the west side of the barracks. As usual, the water was ice cold. Against my hot skin, heated up by the desert heat, the coldness of the water hurt, forcing me to shower as fast as possible. Back in my room, I put on my formal uniform and shined my black leather combat boots with mindful movements. With a 40 degrees Celsius temperature indoors, the shoe shiner had melted into a warm black liquid. Countless flies buzzed around the room, and us, biting our faces and arms, and any exposed skin. As if they knew that this was their last chance for fresh blood; soon we would leave.

We stood straight, waiting for our commanders to arrive for the inspection and let us go on our long-deserved vacations. Suddenly, one of our roommates came rushing in from the shower. We watched how, in a panic, he tripped over and kicked an open can of shoe-shiner across the floor. We gasped and stared, frozen as the can took to the air and splashed its runny, black contents on our uniforms, faces, beds, and the floor. It was like watching a horror scene in slow motion—our spotless presentation ruined. A myriad of emotions washed over me. Shock, numbness, dread, and frustration. Then, the first hoots of laughter started, and soon we were all howling, rolling over, laughing uncontrollably. By now, we were already past the usual inspection time, with the commanders running 5 minutes late, and we knew we were fucked.

Outside, the blue and white buses, our only means of transportation to Tel-Aviv, were parked at the central square. We were impatient and anxious to finish the inspection and go home. Failing would mean a repeat inspection later, and missing the busses. But looking around our room, I realized that no matter how hard we tried to clean everything before inspection, we had no chance of succeeding. We were stuck in the base for the holidays.

Shivta, the location of our base, was in the middle of nowhere in the Negev desert, with no public transportation services or civilian cars on its one-lane road. Especially not on Yom Kippur. The country basically came to a halt.

"Guys, should we try cleaning? They're already late. We might manage," I said, looking from one cadet to another, not convincing even myself.

Some of my friends just shrugged. Then Guy said, "Hey, look. What's going on?" and pointed out the window. Some commanders and instructors stopped their inspections, rushed out from other rooms, and gathered at the base's center square next to the flag. *Why?*

"The buses!" I shouted, as I suddenly noticed them turning on their engines and moving off.

"Where are they going?" Mesika asked, echoing my surprise.

I had hoped the buses were only changing parking locations. But seeing through the opened door the white cloud of dust that raised in their trail, there could be no mistake. The buses had exited the base gates.

"What the hell? They left without us! How will we get home?" I asked, not to anyone in particular.

★★★

"All cadets are ordered immediately to the center square for an announcement!" the loudspeaker boomed with the voice of our company commander.

One by one, the cadets emerged from their rooms and shuffled across the corridors toward the center square in small groups. No one was in a hurry. We'd all understood that our outing was delayed or, even worse, canceled.

One of the instructors ordered us to stand in three lines. He saluted the commander and said, "Sir, all tank commanders' trainees are ready for your commands. Sir."

The company commander waited for our full attention. "No one is leaving for home today. We are on red alert, meaning vacations are off until further notice. Go back to your rooms and change into combat uniforms. You will get an update on any additional information we receive."

"Fuck!" I heard Shaul, who was standing next to me, swear under his breath. "Every time we're about to leave this shithole, something happens."

I nodded. "Yep, here it goes again. Red alert, my ass," I said in frustration. "I had so many plans for these three days."

As a young soldier, I had gotten used to military alerts, especially around holidays, but it hit me hard this time. The training was very intense and challenging, and I was exhausted. I really needed time off.

★★★

On edge, we waited in our room all through the morning. We were tired and disappointed, and the conversation turned to bickering over the army, the canceled vacation, the multitude of flies, and the heat. No one had any news. Nothing happened until the afternoon, when we finally received word from one of the instructors. He stood in the middle of the long corridor, holding a megaphone to his mouth.

"New announcement. All cadets are assigned to tanks as crew members. I posted the list on the newsboard in the hallway. Some of you are to act as tank drivers, others will be positioned as gunners, and some as loaders. The tank commanders are your school instructors."

I checked the list of roles and recognized the cadets in my team but not the assigned commander. His name was Tobi.

I knew all the instructors were skillful commanders. It was a privilege to serve as an instructor in the Academy. The school had chosen the best of the best trainees to continue on as instructors. But Tobi was not one of the instructors I knew. I had never heard of him before.

According to the list, I was the loader, Ron was the driver, and Guy was the gunner. *Great team.* But I wasn't sure about our commander. The survival of the tank team would depend mostly on the commander's fast thinking and decision-making.

"Who is this guy?" I asked Ron, our source for all new rumors.

"He's a captain in the Military Police," Ron said. "He decided to change his career direction and join the Armored Corps. Now he's training for the tank platoon commander position."

Wow! He has just started the process. And since he was already an officer, his training was a fast track through the basics. A shortened version.

I was disturbed by this information. We had been in the Academy for over six months, living and breathing tanks, studying and practicing perfection. And our commander had just arrived a few weeks ago from the Military Police, with limited knowledge and training. Our understanding of operating and commanding a tank was more advanced than his.

"Not even a combat unit!" I said to Ron.

He nodded and whispered, "Fucking military police."

We both knew the score. Only absolute *losers* went to serve there. "Why did we get stuck with this jackass?"

"Who knows? It's probably just another bullshit drill," Ron responded. "Why today of all days, though. That's just sadistic."

I nodded in quiet agreement.

Later in the afternoon, we had a second announcement.

"Cadets, since the kitchen is closed, you'll get a battle ration for lunch, one per crew. At four o'clock, three buses will arrive to take us to Be'er Sheva airport. From there, we'll board a flight to Rephidim. Change your uniform to the Nomex fire protection combat overalls and take all your personal and combat equipment for an extended stay. Pack the rest of your belongings in your kitbags and bring them to the quartermaster's office. And don't forget to mark your names clearly on the bags, so you can find them when you're back here."

"Do you think this is a drill?" I asked Ron and Guy. Their looks told me that the same worries which had begun to sink into my mind were now sinking into theirs. "And where is our commander?" asked Guy.

"Maybe he thought that the crew meant just the driver, gunner, and loader, not the precious tank commander," Ron said.

We shook our heads and chuckled, half despondently. All around us, the other teams gathered in small groups of four to acquaint themselves with one another, bond before departure, and get additional updates from their direct commanders. If this was not a drill, if this was truly real, we were fucked.

★★★

A Hercules carrier aircraft was waiting for us at the airport. We took our stuff from the bus and walked inside the airplane from the drop-back door designed to load heavy military equipment. Two lines of small basket seats were on both sides of the airplane's fuselage, and we sat in an orderly manner. The company commander tallied us to verify that we were all inside.

The door at the back was lifted and closed, and the four massive engines started to rotate their propellers one by one. After less than an hour's flight, we landed in Rephidim in the Sinai desert.

Rephidim was huge, like a small town in the desert, and served as the main frontward operating base for the Air Force, Armored Corps, Supply Corps, and Adjutancy. Buses took us to the armored battalion location of the *Shot-Kal* tanks, just a few kilometers south of the central base.

The base had been vacated by its original tank crews, who had left to reinforce the frontline in the Syrian Golan border the week before. The *Shot-Kal* was equipped with heavy, continuous steel tracks that fitted rocky terrains such as the Syrian border more than the sandy dunes of the Sinai desert. The sand could penetrate into the drive sprocket and throw a track, disabling the tank's maneuvering and exposing it to great danger in combat. The primary designated tanks in the Egyptian frontline were the American *Pattons*. They used rubber pads on their tracks, which worked better on sandy terrain.

Upon arrival at the base, each crew was assigned to a specific tank. We had a long to-do list to complete to bring these machines to full working order. The first task on our hands was to get machine guns from the logistics office, install them in the tanks, and check their calibrations for smooth operation. Then, we continued to prep the monsters for action. We stocked up shells and ammunition and tested the weapon systems. The next step was to refuel and verify oil levels in the engine and transmission. Then, we were to examine the track system, our radio connection, and the turret's electrical systems. The maintenance and service tools were placed in order at the external tank bins. Finally, we filled our jerrycans with freshwater and organized our personal stuff.

We worked all night long and looked on in envy at all the other crews working together with their commanders as a team. Our commander, Tobi, arrived early the following day, after we had finished, to drop in his personal stuff and ask if all the tasks were completed.

Finally, we could get some sleep. Except for a short nap, I hadn't slept much in the past 48 hours.

We went to the logistics tent, signed, and received paper-thin mattresses, sleeping bags, and one wool blanket each. Then, we looked for our company's tents. They were well organized in a half-circle shape, with four tents for the crews, one for the officers, and one for the company commander and deputy.

Most of the army cots inside the tents were already occupied, as we were the last crew to complete all its tasks.

I placed the mattress on top of the metal-framed bed, covered it with the blanket, and then sat down to remove my boots. *Oh!* What a relief it was. I crawled into my sleeping bag, still wearing my Nomex overall as we were still under high alert. Wrapping my Uzi gun with my coat, I placed it under my head, used it as a pillow, and immediately drifted off into a deep sleep.

Shot-Kal tank. (Wikimedia)

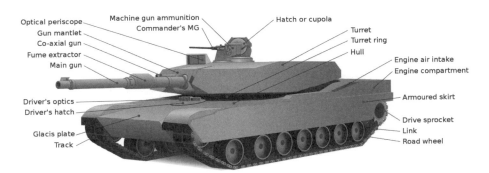

The key parts of a battle tank. (Wikimedia)

CHAPTER 2

The First Day of the Yom Kippur War, October 6, 1973

"Wake up! Wake up!" I heard someone shouting outside the tent.

"Wake up! You will redeploy before sunrise. Be ready to move in fifteen minutes," the sentry shouted. "Change into your combat Nomex uniforms and follow your platoon commander to your destination. All tanks must be covered with a camouflage net. And from now on, we are in total radio silence."

"Shit. I hardly slept! Maybe two hours in total," I said to Ron.

"Yeah, me too, and now not only do we need to handle these filthy, dusty nets, we also need to move the tanks to spread out as if it's an effective way of hiding them. What bullshit!" Ron retorted.

And Guy added, "Besides, there's no real threat. What are the chances that enemy fighter jets will get here? We're far off the Egyptian frontline and have the best air force in the Middle East to protect our borders."

"Also," I jumped in, "Nearby, we've got the most sophisticated ground-to-air missile base to defend Rephidim."

Placing the camouflage net over the tank was one of the most hated drills. We'd practiced it repeatedly, especially when our instructors wanted to punish us. The crews had to complete these tasks within five minutes. That was exhausting. It covered us with dust and sand and filled the tank with these dirt particles. Whenever you wanted to enter, or get something from the outside storage bins, you had to crawl under that filthy net and get dirty yourself.

I quickly packed my sleeping bag, folded my blanket, and rolled my mattress, and carried all to our tank, where I tied it to the open external

The author's tank under a camouflage net.

storage basket. Then I climbed into my loader cell. Ron and Guy were already waiting inside. Our commander, Tobi, was nowhere in sight.

"He will probably show up just before the company commander arrives," Ron said.

Ron was right. Tobi arrived at the very last moment, asking off-handedly, "Is everyone here? Are you all ready to move?"

"Yes," we said.

Gila company began moving slowly. The first tank was that of the company commander, and one by one, the other tanks followed. We were tank 3A, which meant we were the eighth tank to join the convoy. The company had a total of 11 tanks. After a few minutes, the company commander stopped his tank and signaled the three platoons, with flags, to their exact locations.

Our platoon commander stopped and flagged our tank to our place.

We rolled the camouflage net down both sides of the tank until it covered the tank completely. To change the silhouette of the tank, we stuck cannons cleaning rods, shovels, and a few jerrycans between the body and the net.

We pulled the net further over on the west side of the tank to make a shaded seating area. The sun climbed high in the sky and heated the desert, but sitting under our makeshift canopy was pleasant and refreshing.

Now we have time to rest.

I climbed up on the tank under the net, opened one of the general external storage bins, and found my toiletries in my backpack. I washed the sand off my face and hair, brushed my teeth, and shaved the stubble around my mouth. I believed that repeated shaving would speed up the growth of my facial hair and would give me the look of an adult man.

The break didn't last long.

Around noon, a new announcement came from our company commander. "We received a radio transmission. This evening, we will join the combat. I expect to get our mission and orders shortly. Remove the camouflage net off the loader machinegun, and arrange guard shifts for each tank around the clock."

I was so surprised. The whole situation made no sense to me. None at all.

We flipped a coin between the three of us, as our commander was nowhere to be seen. We assumed he wouldn't share any crew duties since he was *the officer*. All other teams shared tasks evenly. Just the way it should be.

We really have no luck with our commander.

I got the first shift. I collected my Uzi, my military gear and two water bottles, and climbed to the top of the turret underneath the netting. At my post in the loader cell, I opened the net to expose the 0.3" Browning machine gun and loaded it with ammunition. Wearing the helmet for emergency radio communications, I grabbed my binoculars, stood on the loader chair, and looked around. All the other tanks were doing the same. Each tank had a guard on duty.

Nothing to watch. Just a typical desert. As far as the eye could see, yellow, sun-bleached sand dunes spread across the horizon. Above, a bright blue sky with the sun blazing so hard, you could hardly keep your eyes open. *Boring.*

Suddenly, as I was waiting to be released from my guard duty, noisy, roaring fighter jets appeared in the sky, flying incredibly low above us.

Are these our Kfir *jets practicing? It can't be anything else*, I thought.

"Those are Egyptian jets!" I heard someone shout.

What? Can it be? They passed straight above us without shooting. No warning messages on the radio. They must be our jets.

I watched as two of the four planes changed direction and steered toward the Hawk missile battery. The other two went toward Rephidim airport and the central base.

Moments later, flashes of lights followed by giant, gray mushrooms of smoke were visible from the airport and the missile battery.

Then, we heard thunderous sounds.

BOOM!!!

BOOM!!!

BOOM!!!

The earth shook underneath us as the jets bombed our antiaircraft missile battery, the military base, and the airport. I didn't see any response from our forces. Not from the Hawk missiles, or the central army base—Rephidim, or the airfield.

How can this happen? This is not what I expected. Not in a million years!

★★★

We had grown up on stories of soldiers' heroism. We were raised in the deep belief that Israel had the mightiest and bravest army in our hostile neighborhood. Since the Six-Day War, when we had crushed our enemies—Egypt, Syria, and Jordan—in just a few days, we had trusted our air force to be the best in the Middle East. And we had trusted our pilots—the most skilled—to shoot down any aggressive attempts to enter our airspace. Our leaders had repeatedly promised us that we had the newest, most sophisticated missile defense capability to destroy any adversary power within our borders. The Arab soldiers were seen as weak and cowardly to fight against the IDF—the Israel Defense Force.

Then how could Egyptian fighter jets reach here, within the midst of our territory, flying hundreds of kilometers within our borders to attack us?

★★★

"They are coming back. Fire at will!" the radio suddenly came alive.

The planes passed above us, still at low altitude, rushing back to Egypt. Some of the tanks tried shooting with their machine guns. I looked up at the aircraft getting further away and watched for any sign of smoke, damage, or engine failure, but saw nothing.

The chance of hitting a fighter jet with a machine gun was near zero. *What now?* I was baffled.

A few minutes later, our platoon commander came running and called us to gather in front of his tank.

"Platoon Three, I have updated orders. Remove the camouflage nets and be ready to move. The Egyptian army is attacking our positions at the Bar-Lev line. Our soldiers there need our immediate support. We will drive on tracks to the central sector of the Bar-Lev line and help them keep the frontlines as required. Then we will cross the Egyptians' bridges and go straight to Cairo. There are no more instructions, for now. Let's get ready ASAP."

What??? Have they already built bridges? What about our "secret plan"?

The plot, known to all, was to set the Suez Canal on fire, using a massive oil reservoir which we would pump into the canal.

We returned to our tank, folded back the camouflage net, entered our cells, and put on our helmets.

Tobi, our commander, arrived too. "We're going to war. Hurry up, let's start moving," he said in excitement.

I did a quick calculation. The distance to the Bar-Lev line was about 100 kilometers. If we drove at an average speed of 20 kilometers per hour, it would take us four to five hours to reach our destination.

The tanks started moving forward, and each entered the convoy in sequence. The lead tank was the company commander, followed by Platoons One, Two, and Three. The company deputy commander's tank closed the convoy.

"Gila Stations, this is Gila Sunray; do you hear me? Over," asked our company commander.

Tank by tank answered: "Sound clear."

"Proceed in combat progressing patterns. Out."

The tanks moved from a single, straight line to a wide-open diamond pattern, creating a massive dust cloud in the process.

I stood up tall by the side of our commander, wearing my fancy pair of dust goggles to protect my eyes from the heavy dust. They were a special gift from my parents. After seeing my red eyes over one of my vacations, they'd put much effort and time into buying me these expensive dust-protective glasses.

The standard IDF dust goggles were hard plastic that didn't seal well to protect the eyes from the dust.

I knew my duties as a loader. I was to stand up on top of the loader chair, with my head and chest above the loader hatch, and help my commander, Tobi, navigate and detect obstacles in our way. In case of a sudden attack, I would load the weapon systems with the proper ammo or use the machine gun in front of me.

Ron was driving the tank with the driver lid closed and using his periscopes to keep the correct distance and position from the tanks around us. He was an excellent driver, drove the armored vehicle safely and responsibly, and didn't need many direction corrections from Tobi.

Guy, the gunner, was the lucky one. He could rest during the drive, as there was nothing to do, even though his duty was to search for threats through his periscope.

"Tobi, can I open the lid and lift my driver's chair to better see the road?" Ron asked.

"No! Drive with the lid closed," Tobi answered.

I could feel Ron's frustration. To drive the tank with a closed lid meant having a limited view and depending on your commander's orders.

What's his problem? We have about four hours of driving along the main road until we get to the war zone. Maneuvering with the lid closed is a nightmare for any driver.

Most of the other tanks drove with their tops opened.

I looked around. There was nothing around us but dust and a monotonous desert view. Nothing much was happening; even the radio was silent. After three hours of driving west, we reached 'Hatam' road, a narrow north-south road that crossed dunes and sandy terrain, and ran parallel to the Suez Canal. It was constructed to support the Bar-Lev line, whose primary purpose was to block the Egyptian army from crossing the canal.

"Move on the road, I repeat, on the road," the battalion commander ordered.

That was strange. Our tanks had naked steel chains that would dig into the soft asphalt and destroy the costly road. *We must be in a real rush!*

Driving on those dunes alongside the road would slow us down and might throw a track, which would force the affected tank to stop for repairs.

Maybe things aren't going so well at the frontline, and we must get there sooner rather than later, no matter the cost. My heart sank with my thoughts.

In front of us, tank after tank climbed on the asphalt road. Ron turned the tank 45 degrees toward the road, and keeping that angle, we slowly climbed on the asphalt. When the tank reached the center of the road, Ron turned the tank in the direction of the convoy.

The tanks moved fast on the tarmac. A gust of wind blew across my face, and the nasty sand stopped bothering me. It was a good feeling; a rush of adrenaline coursed through my body, and I felt like a mighty knight riding his noble beast, ready for battle.

Suddenly, our tank steered off to the right side of the road and started sliding into a deep, sandy ditch. It tilted sideways, with one track on the asphalt and the other in the sand.

Ron slowed down and turned the tank toward the dune's direction.

"Left! Turn left," Tobi shouted into the internal communications.

Ron shouted back, "No, we'll throw the track."

He was right. In such a situation, as we learned in the Academy, the driver controlled the tank movement by staying in the same position and pulling slightly to the right.

Tobi was furious. His face turned red.

"How dare you? Pull hard left! That is an order," Tobi shot out his words.

Ron obeyed and pulled the steering wheel hard to the left. A sickening screech came from the track, like the sound of a wounded animal.

Tobi yelled yet another command. "Full gas."

And that was it. The tank stopped moving.

"Move the tank. Full gas ahead."

Ron tried, and the engine screamed, but the tank didn't move. Not even an inch.

Tobi was beside himself with rage. "You! Stupid driver! Why aren't we moving?"

We knew right away what had just happened. The tank now sat in the sandy ditch in a 30 degrees side tilt with a thrown track.

Ron answered in a dry, emotionless voice, "We probably have a thrown track."

"Gila Sunray, this is 3A. We have a minor technical problem that has forced us to stop. Over," Tobi said to the company commander.

"I got your message. Repair and join us ASAP. Out," the commander answered over the radio.

We climbed down to assess the damage. It was a badly thrown track. It lay under the tank's belly, stretched to breaking point at the front.

Ron took the required tools—a 5 kilogram hammer, a steel rod, an enormous track tensioning spanner, and a special rope. The standard practice was to complete up to 20 full turns of the tensioning nut to release the tension. Then, to unlock and separate two links and place them flat on the ground, and with the rope, put the tracks back in place and connect the open links. The final step was to adjust them to the correct tension.

But nothing worked as usual. We tried everything, but the track was still stretched too tight. It was hot, about 40 degrees Celsius. Ron, Guy, and I were working to exhaustion while our commander, Tobi, stood on his chair at the turret and watched over us.

Finally, just when we thought we had released the tension successfully, the track snapped with a cracking noise and locked the steel rod inside the links.

"We are fucked!" Ron said. "Now we don't have any tools to open the track."

With a sneering expression, Tobi called the company commander to request support from the first-level maintenance squad. They arrived shortly after and assessed the situation.

"Nothing we can do. This is a bad throw; you need second-level support to cut one of the links with a welder and open the track. I'll call them, but they won't come until tomorrow morning. The road is completely closed off for the night," the mechanic said. "You guys, be careful. We got radio communications warning us about Egyptian commando forces swarming around."

"What???" Ron asked. "How can we protect ourselves? The tank is stuck, tilted at 30 degrees in the ditch, which means our machineguns can't shoot to the west in the direction of the commandos."

The mechanic looked at him and just shrugged. "Use your Uzis," he said as he turned to his jeep. "Good luck, soldiers." He waved his hand in goodbye.

"What bullshit!" I called in frustration. "The commandos have AK-47s, and our Uzis are no match for them. But, you know what, Ron, I'm sure he exaggerated. Our battalion should arrive at the Suez Canal soon and beat the Egyptian army up," I said confidently. *But was I?*

It turned dark. The traffic on the road stopped, just as the mechanic warned us it would. Our only method of communicating with the departing company—the radio—had gone silent. We had no signal except for static bursts now and then, as we were out of their range. We started getting ready for the night. Our best protection in that situation was to hide in the ditch, eliminate any light, and keep quiet. I turned the radio off to reduce the static noises and save battery life.

The desert night was dark. No moon, no stars, only silence and loneliness. Nobody else was around.

Our mood was gloomy. The tension, like the gap between us, the cadets, and Tobi, just widened. No one tried to break the ice. *It's going to be a long, long night.* "I'm an officer and have other crucial duties on my hands," Tobi said when we talked about guard shifts. We exchanged side glances but had no choice. We split the schedule between us three; Ron got the first shift, me the second, and Guy was the lucky last. He could sleep for a long, uninterrupted period.

I turned off all the lights inside the turret. I could hear the faint sound of explosions from the west and could see flares dropping slowly from the sky, along with flashes of lights. It was like viewing a heavy thunderstorm far in the distance. We were all alone.

We each opened our battle rations. The box contained one can of sweetcorn kernels, a tin of goulash stew, a small box of Halva, a tin of sardines, a packet of crackers, and a can of sliced pineapple. We gobbled everything down as it was, cold. We ate fast, and quietly.

"Hey, Amir, wake up. It's almost two o'clock. Nothing happened," Ron said as he touched my shoulder. "I'll wait until you are ready to start your shift."

I exited my loader hatch, where I had been snoozing while sitting on my chair.

Ron verified I was fully awake and alert and standing on my feet on top of the chair in front of the loader machine gun before he went to sleep in his cell.

I checked if the machine gun was loaded and in safe mode. Then I took my Uzi from beside me, loaded it with a magazine, set it on safety, and put on my combat webbing and helmet.

Looking around, I couldn't see anything. I raised my binoculars, yet saw no movement around our tank. The night was quiet except for low, monotonous noises. Maybe it was the wind blowing away dead, dried bushes, owls hooting in the distance, or perhaps the sound of the desert breathing. We were all alone here, and I was nervous.

It was dark, and I turned my eyes up to the sky. The moon came out from behind the clouds. Millions of stars were spread above us like a vast canopy of bright, shimmering, beautiful diamonds. I had always been fascinated by the stars; they had a magical existence beyond my understanding. Their incredible magnitude and eternity gave me a constant sense of calmness and reduced my anxiety. I recognized the North Star, the Big Dipper, and the Little Dipper. They were sparkling, shining far away in their peaceful, protected space, as if asking, *"What is wrong with you people, down there?"*

★★★

What is wrong with us people, down here? Why do we need to defend our lives time and again? We, the Israelis, are good people, helping everybody, and spreading the light to the world.

We had learned that in history classes, in social studies, at home, and in youth organizations. Our history extended from biblical times to the modern era, centuries of hardship and misery. We had been scattered all around the globe without a place to call home. From exile to the torture of the Inquisition, from restrictions of occupation, of residency, to deportation and expulsions, and the holocaust, the murdering of six million Jews in an attempt to exterminate the Jewish people. The Zionist movement, which had started at the end of the

19th century, recognized that the Jewish people must return to their biblical homeland, the land of Israel. The land that God had promised to our father, Abraham.

After WWII, many Jewish youths, like my parents, immigrated to the new State of Israel, an abandoned place of swamps, deserts, and wilderness, and turned this desert into a flourishing, thriving garden of Eden. They drained the marshlands to combat malaria, built villages, kibbutzim, and cities, paved roads, and planted trees for the well-being of all residents of this country—Jews, Muslims, Druzes, and Christians.

Because of our tragic experiences, we treated all minorities with compassion and respect. We gave them equal rights as Israeli citizens. The few hundred Arab residents in the West Bank and Gaza Strip refugee camps had decided to flee their villages in Israel instead of living amongst us. That was their choice.

Then why, for God's sake, is Egypt attacking us? They have no reason to war with us. The Sinai desert we captured in the Six-Day War in 1967 doesn't really belong to them. Nobody lives here except for a few Bedouin tribes.

My thoughts went in circles, unable to understand why the Arab countries at our borders hated us so much and wished to destroy our state and kill us. We had showed them we could all live good and prosperous lives and fulfill our dreams. Yet they had chosen war, time after time.

And understanding we had no choice but to go to war for the sake of our country filled me with renewed determination.

I will protect and fight the best I can. The alternative is the destruction of my homeland and the deaths of our people, including my family. To sacrifice my life for my country would be an honorable death, and I am willing to offer it.

★★★

It was still quiet around us. The bitter cold of the desert hardened the tank's steel body in a brutal and unforgiving way. I paid a painful price in bruises for any careless moves.

In the distance, I could still see the flashing of lights and hear the rumbling sounds of the war in the west. Mixed with the noise of the cold wind against my face and the chirping of crickets, I didn't feel any immediate threat.

CHAPTER 3

Facing Reality, October 7, 1973

The eastern skyline started to light up and began to glow in a reddish haze. A thin red–orange arc rose slowly above the horizon and quickly turned into a round ball of fire that dissolved the desert cold. It warmed up the frozen steel and gently caressed my cold cheeks. But, as the sun climbed higher and grew warmer, I knew the weather would soon turn scorching hot.

I wondered about all my friends from the Academy. *They have probably crossed the Suez Canal and are far away from us already.*

The noise of a military convoy on the road got my attention. I looked through my binoculars and identified a force approaching us, driving north on Hatam Road.

"They're IDF forces. Our people!" I said to my crew, feeling happy and relieved.

A small, armored infantry unit rushed north without slowing down. Tobi told me to turn on the radio and try to contact them. But they were using their radio channel frequency, and no one was listening to the emergency frequency.

A few military jeeps passed by us, speeding up, not bothering to check on us. At 8:00 a.m., I heard another convoy. I lifted my binoculars to my eyes and looked to see if it was a threat before identifying them as another convoy of IDF armored vehicles. One of them carried a large crane for lifting heavy cars.

"The second line of the maintenance support group is approaching us," I announced. *Finally, we will be out of here, rejoining our friends.* I wanted to talk with my roommates and see how they were doing and if our company and battalion were safe after last night.

The support team officer stopped next to our tank and evaluated the damage to determine the best repair method.

"What the hell did you do? Don't you know that you can't turn the tank against the sliding direction if you're sliding on a dune?" He looked at us, unhappy. "First, you must turn the tank to the tilt direction and then, slowly, roll back to the road." He taught us the basics of tank driving skills, which we had all learned in the Academy for the past six months, except for Tobi.

Tobi interjected, "This is the work of my stupid driver. He's useless!"

I could see Ron's face changing color from pale to deep red, but he didn't utter a word and kept his thoughts to himself.

The support commander looked at Tobi and didn't respond to his nasty words. I thought he must have known that this damage was the tank commander's responsibility, not the driver's.

He turned to his team and gave them detailed instructions: "Cut the track, remove the link, replace it with a new one, and pull it back around the wheels and the drive sprocket."

They started to braze one of the links at the bottom, just below the drive sprocket. It broke with a loud bang, releasing the pressure which had built up inside. That was the fastest way to open the links and put the track back in place. In a few minutes, the repair work was completed.

The tank was ready for us. We entered inside, each of us going to our designated cell. I turned the radio on, plugged my helmet into the radio network, and connected myself to the internal communications. Tobi asked if we were ready to go, and each of us answered, "Yes, Sir!"

Ron turned on the ignition switch, and the tank woke up with a roar like a wild beast boasting its strength, trying to prove its trustworthiness, as if saying, "You can fully rely on me; no one can stop us. We are a mighty powerful machine-human hybrid."

"Driver, get us back on the road," Tobi said to Ron, but didn't specify how to maneuver the tank.

Ron put the transmission on the drive, took a half-circle turn in the direction of the dunes, and slowly turned the tank back to the road.

We were finally back on the road, speeding up north toward the estimated location of our battalion, which was too far away from the radio range.

I was standing on my chair with my upper body exposed above the turret for better viewing. This was the tradition of the Iron Men.

"Tank commanders and loaders do not hide inside the turrets with closed hatches, like chickens in their coop. We are IDF fighters, and we are fearless!" That awareness was preached to us at the Armored Corps, day in and day out. The commander and the loader stood straight above the turret, exposed from their waist up during tank maneuvering. The higher that one was mounted, the better it was.

The tank was traveling at full speed, the wind was cooling my face, and I felt like I was galloping on the beast's back toward our big victory. *We are so powerful.*

We drove north for about half an hour, and then, suddenly, the radio woke up. It started receiving broken messages on the company network.

"They must be nearby," Tobi said in excitement. He tried to call our company commander again and again.

"Gila Sunray, this is 3A. Do you copy? Over." The radio reverted to static background noise.

"Gila Sunray, this is 3A. Do you copy? Over."

"Sunray, Sunray, Sunray! This is 3A, ready to join the company. Over."

Yet, no answer. "This is 3A from Gila Company; can anyone hear me? Over."

Suddenly, we received a response. "This is Barak Sunray. Your company radio frequency is no longer active. Connect to the Barak network for instructions. Out."

I was surprised. *What the hell is going on? Why do we have to contact our battalion commander directly? Where is my company?*

Tobi instructed me to change our network channel to the frequency used by the Barak network and called immediately. "Barak, this is 3A of Gila. Do you copy? Over."

"Copy, 3A of Gila. You sound clear. Join our forces at Tirtur and Lexicon on your code map. Out."

"Barak, this is 3A of Gila. Wilco. Over."

"Stop the tank," Tobi ordered Ron, and dived into the turret to find the code map Sirius and the locations.

It wasn't far from our position.

A few minutes later, we got close to the gathering point. It was 11:00 a.m., a clear day, but smoke rose from the horizon in the west. I saw a few *Shot-Kal* tanks, which seemed like they had belonged to our battalion, scattered over a flat, white sand plateau and guarded by armored infantry. I tried to identify my company but couldn't. In total, there were only five tanks from our three companies.

It didn't seem right.

Where are all our companies? Maybe these five tanks are assembled here on a special task force with the battalion commander.

Tobi called them over the radio. "Barak, this is 3A of Gila. Do you copy? Over."

"We're on full radio silence," was the immediate response.

Tobi told Ron to approach the tank marked "10", the battalion commander's tank. Our tank glided over the small, sandy hills until we reached the spot next to the commander.

All the other tanks were spread about 100 meters apart from each other. Their teams looked exhausted. No one talked, smiled, or welcomed us with a wave. They lay on the sand in the shaded area alongside the tanks, staring straight at us, motionless, without acknowledging our arrival.

Ron turned the engine off, and we all climbed down.

Tobi approached the battalion commander, "Where is my company?" he asked.

"This is all that's left of our battalion force after last night's battle," the commander answered in a broken voice. "We gathered here, and from now on, we'll act as one small unit under my command. We no longer need a battalion structure for such a small force."

Shit! What happened? We're the mighty IDF Iron Fist! We were supposed to cross the Egyptian bridge fast and storm directly into Cairo without resistance. Now, all that is left are the six tanks out of the 36 we started with yesterday! And with this fraction of our battalion, do we need to stop the Egyptians' progress and defend our lines? How could we have lost 30 tanks in one night?

I stared at the commander in disbelief. *What a disaster!*

And each tank has a crew of four. I started to calculate in my head. *Where are the 120 crew members of the lost tanks?*

Where are all my friends? What happened to them?

Are they dead? Wounded? Missing? Captured?

Where are my friends?

They were my buddies, with whom I had shared my life over the past six months. We had trained together, shared meals, packages of treats we got from home, and personal stories about girlfriends we'd left behind. We joked, complained, faced challenges and difficulties in the classroom and training, and always supported each other on any occasion.

These are my brothers!

One by one, their faces flashed through my mind as I wondered about their fate. I choked back the tears in my throat.

How can this have happened?

What a blow!

I stood next to Ron and Guy, who looked as shocked as me by the news. Nobody talked. There was nothing to say.

The battalion commander sent his crew to gather everybody around his tank for a quick briefing. He looked at us with a dark, serious expression. "We're the only force in the area that can stop or slow down the Second Army from moving into the Sinai Peninsula toward the Mitle and Gidi passages and into Israel," he said quietly. "Our reserve units are not ready yet. Their call-up had started, but it would take them at least forty-eight hours to get here. We must do everything we can to halt the Egyptian army and buy some time for the sake of our nation." He paused to let us comprehend the gravity of the situation. But what he said next was even more unnerving.

"I want to review the lessons learned from last night's battle. Listen carefully. The lives of all of us depend on following these recommendations. Our main threats are the commando and infantry squads. They're using portable, antitank guided Sagger missiles with a firing range of up to 3,000 meters, similar to our maximum. They are connected to a small-sized box with two wires, carried by the operator, and are accurate. The soldier will lie down, hide behind dunes, detect the target through binoculars, and fire. You won't see him or the missile."

It's impossible to spot the launch point at this range!
The commander continued.

"These are the tactics we must take to defend ourselves.

1. You can't see the missile when it's heading toward you, but the tank next to you or the infantry at the outer sides of our battalion will be able to detect it and warn the force.
2. Since it's a slow-moving missile, you'll have a few seconds to change position after the warning.
3. Before climbing to the firing position, every tank must verify that it has a lookout on its side to warn of upcoming missiles.
4. Anyone spotting a missile will cut in Barak's radio network to warn everybody. Use the code 'approaching missile.'
5. Drivers, upon hearing the warning, immediately move back from the fire position to a lookout or full hide position. If you can't find the proper place for your tank, release a smoke grenade to hide it. But consider wind direction before throwing the grenade."

"And lastly..." he paused, "I don't need to tell you how to do combat. Remember that we are the best soldiers in the world, and we proved it yesterday. Be brave, and may God be with us and with Israel."

His words, grave and solemn, struck a chord in my heart, and a surge of adrenaline ran through my body. I pulled back my shoulders and straightened my back. *Yes, that's us. The best and the bravest.*

★★★

Ron, Guy, and I returned to our tank while Tobi stayed with the battalion officers to get more information.

"What the fuck is going on?" Ron said. "In my worst nightmare, I wouldn't think this could happen. We're the best tank teams and the best performers in the tank training school. The Academy commanders and trainers are well-chosen sergeants and officers! And now, they're defeated by the stinking Egyptian army?" His voice rose a notch, and he paused to get a hold of his emotions. "Except for our tank commander, the loser who arrived from the Military Police...," he said bitterly.

"Yeah, I know. It's awful," I said. "And what's the story with these missiles? We've not heard about them before."

Front View of a Tank in Turret-down and Hull-down positions. A vehicle in a position with a background is more difficult to observe than one which is skylined. (Wikiwand)

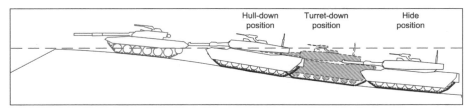

Tank tactical positions. (Wikimedia)

We had learned many details about the enemy's tanks, about identifying them, and differentiating between the T-54, T-55, and T-62, supplied by the USSR. We recognized the antitank cannons, the antitank weapons like the RPG, which the commandos and infantry used, and how to prioritize enemy targets by the harm they could inflict on us. We had

had to write many exams on these subjects. But we'd been told nothing about antitank missiles like the Sagger.

"Did the military, the intelligence, just miss them? These are way more dangerous than any of the tanks we learned about," I said, frustrated.

"It's like fighting blindfolded. You can't detect them, but they can hit your tank without exposing themselves," Guy added. "That could explain last night's disaster and the loss of our tanks in just a few hours. Our friends wouldn't have even know what hit them and where it came from. They couldn't have protected themselves. They were just cannon fodder," he said in anger.

I looked at him and asked, "What do you mean? Why do you say that?"

"Because nobody had warned us before about these missiles; they were sent into this war with no chance of survival or of gaining any advantage, and they paid for it with their lives. As I said, cannon fodder."

"Those are tough words, Guy," I said.

It was hard for me to hear, and I climbed back into the tank turret to find a packet of biscuits. I've always found comfort in eating when stressed. It had been a lifelong battle to control my weight and keep my military uniform in size medium while most of my friends wore size small. I took the biscuits down to share with Ron and Guy, sitting in the shaded area by the tank tracks.

The exhaustion of the last couple of days had taken its toll on us, and we started to nap.

"Wake up, wake up," Tobi was shouting. "We're leaving soon to stop the Egyptians' progress west toward the Gidi passage."

Tobi sounded excited, like a kid looking forward to a great adventure. "Gunner, get in immediately," Toby rushed Guy to enter inside the turret, so that he could stand on his commander's chair, above the gunner seat, ready to follow the battalion commander's orders.

Ron entered the driver cell, and I climbed quickly to the loader chamber, stood on my chair, and put on my helmet which was connected to the radio system.

Tobi checked the status of the internal communications system. "How do you hear me?" he asked.

We answered in order, "Sound clear, Sir."

"Barak station," the battalion commander's voice came through the radio. "This is Barak Sunray. Follow me in battle structure and keep the radio network in silent mode. In an emergency, break into radio silence."

The battalion commander started moving, and the five tanks followed him in a diamond shape.

Tobi told Ron, "Follow the tank marked number two. Our position is to its left and behind. Keep about a 100 meter distance."

"Wilco," Ron replied.

Fifteen minutes later, the battalion commander placed us behind a few low hills facing the west, at a hidden position. Suddenly, the radio silence was broken.

"This is Barak Sunray," the battalion commander said. "We're about to confront the Egyptian forces moving toward us. The range for the first contact will be about 2,000 to 3,000 meters. Look for tanks and be on the watch for commando and infantry missiles."

He then addressed our infantry support forces. They were called Sugar. "Sugar Sunray, this is Barak Sunray. Position yourself at the two far sides of the hills, north and south of our tanks, at surveillance, and alert the tanks to missile launches. Out to you."

The commander's next orders addressed us. "This is Barak Sunray to tanks 1, 1B, 2, 2A, 3A. Fire only on my command. Keep the tanks at the turret-down position to protect yourselves. Rise to hull-down position only after identifying the enemy and being ready to fire. Fire to kill. Stay in hull-down for the shortest time possible and back off to turret-down the moment you finish shooting. Don't use the same spot for your next hull-down. We'll work in pairs, Barak Sunray with 1, 2 with 2A, and 1B with 3A. Acknowledge."

The answers came one by one from each tank:

"Wilco 1."

"Wilco 1B."

"Wilco 2."

"Wilco 2A."

"Wilco 3A."

"Wilco Sugar."

We moved to turret-down position behind a low dune hill and next to 1B, to watch and identify the enemy. Tobi and I stood as high as we could on our chairs, binoculars fixed to our eyes. We looked for any movement in front of us, watching to identify the Egyptian forces. The dune protected our tanks, and only our heads were exposed to the direction of the enemy.

The area was a typical Sinai desert landscape. Yellow dunes, dwarf bushes, and a few acacia trees that had survived the dry, hot sun, which now torched us from high in the sky.

I couldn't see any vehicle, tank, infantry, or commando forces in front of us. I used my 8×30 binoculars to detect any movement in the distance, but detected nothing, no potential threats.

Suddenly, the radio broke its silence. "This is Barak Sunray. Your target is 3,000 meters to the front, at one o'clock. Look for movement, identify your target, and fire at will. Out to you."

Tobi's face broke into a wide smile. "Check, check. Can you see anything?" he asked me.

"No, not yet."

"Look again. I'm sure there's something around that acacia tree ahead of us," he said. Suddenly, I heard him over the internal communication network. "Driver, go ahead."

I was surprised. *What the hell is he doing?*

★★★

As cadets, we'd known the firing commands by heart, practicing them hundreds of times during our intensive training as tank commanders.

First, the commander had to give a pre-fire command while the tank was still at a turret-down position and unexposed to enemy fire. That was crucial, as it provided the team with all the necessary information to prepare the systems for firing before moving to hull-down position.

The pre-fire command included the following information: the weapon we intended to use—cannon or machine gun; the type of ammunition to use when the cannon was selected; the estimated direction and range of the target, i.e., at two o'clock 2,500 meters; and a short description of the target, like whether it was a tank, an armored vehicle, infantry, etc.

Each crew member prepared the tank systems to execute the fire command.

The gunner would set the firing system according to the type of ammo and the range of the target.

At the same time, the loader would load the ammo into the gun and prepare additional shells.

The driver would then shift gears to drive and hold the brakes, ready to take the hull-down position.

When the crew was confirmed and ready, the tank commander gave the driver the command to go ahead and stopped him at a hull-down position.

The gunner aimed the gun at the target and announced, "On."

The commander approved and ordered, "Fire."

The gunner replied, "Shooting," and released the first shell.

After completing the fire sequence, the tank would immediately return to the safe turret-down position and search for a new target. The less the tank stayed at hull-down, the greater the chance of survival.

★★★

Ron was hesitant to respond.

Tobi shouted, "Driver, go!"

Ron started the tank and moved forward slowly. I waited for Tobi to give the order to stop at the turret-down position, but it never happened, and soon, we were totally up the dune, exposed from top to bottom. An easy target for the Egyptians to destroy.

"I can see the killing zone in front of me. We're fully exposed!" Ron called over our radio communications.

I heard the urgency in his voice, which only angered Tobi who snapped, "This is not an insurance policy. It is a war."

His response was as shocking to me as I'm sure it was for Ron and Guy. *He has no clue how to command a tank, and we are like sitting ducks in the kill zone.*

Tobi couldn't hide his excitement. "Do you see the target near the acacia tree?" he asked Guy, our gunner, and turned the main gun toward that direction.

"I'm not sure. Maybe there are a few soldiers over there," Guy answered.

"Fire, fire," Tobi shouted.

"What ammo do you want to use?" I asked.

"What is the range?" Guy asked.

Tobi immediately barked, "APDS, 3,000 meters."

I loaded the APDS shell into the gun and said, "Loaded."

"APDS is armor-piercing and is not good for soft targets," Guy said.

Tobi ignored him and ordered loudly, "Fire."

Guy released the first shell and the piercing head hit the dune sand, but it was short of the target, causing no damage.

Suddenly, a long shiver crawled down my spine. A sickening sensation rose in the pit of my stomach, telling me something terrible was going to happen to us soon. Very soon. Deep inside me, I knew that a missile would strike us. I had no doubts! But where will it hit? The front? The back of the tank? My brain processed the unknown quickly, trying to figure it out.

Then, I knew. It would hit the back of the tank. I squashed myself into the co-axial machine gun inside the front of the turret.

BOOM!

The 50-tonne tank shook like a leaf in stormy wind.

I can't see.

I can't hear.

I don't feel anything.

Am I dead?

I lifted my arms and touched my face. I could feel my face. *No, I wasn't dead.* I opened my eyes; it was dark inside the turret. I started to pat down my body, limb by limb, from my legs up to my hips, stomach, and chest, verifying that I was intact and okay. A buzzing noise screamed in my ears.

The tank was full of heavy, sickening smoke inside the turret. Smoke was also billowing outside at its back. Ron immediately shifted the gear to reverse to get us to a protected area behind the dune, but the tank didn't move. It was dead.

The tanks around us started to return fire to protect and rescue us. 1B, next to us, approached immediately to assess the damage.

"We need to tow you out of the killing zone," the commander of 1B said. "Prepare the cables, and we'll come back." He turned quickly and moved to a turret-down position as before.

A barrage of artillery dropped all around, but it landed far away from us and was unprecise.

Tobi ordered me, "Get down and connect the towing cables to the front shackles."

I was pissed off with him. *I can't ask him to move his ass and help me. He's an officer! Probably thinks it's safer inside or that it's not his job.*

I climbed down. The back of the tank was still smoking but there wasn't any visible fire. The extinguishers had been activated automatically.

The tank had two heavyweight steel towing cables hooked around its rear end. Removing them, straightening them in front of the tank, and connecting them to the shackles in a cross shape was a strenuous and time-consuming job to carry out alone. At the Academy, we always practiced towing procedures in pairs.

I started with the first cable. It was boiling hot outside and the white sandy ground added friction, making the wire towing rope even harder to pull. Sweat dripped down my face and along my back. Finally, I finished with the first cable. I rested for a few moments to catch my breath and recover from the grueling process before tackling the second cable.

Tobi, who didn't move from the turret, was impatient. "Quickly, quickly, the artillery is coming closer. Do you want to die?"

I continued and connected the second one in place. That took me even longer as I was exhausted. Finally, I was done and signaled 1B to come closer. The tank approached immediately, and I connected the cables to its tow shackles and guided the driver to move slowly until the two wires were aligned and stretched. At this stage, any fast movement would snap the cables. I climbed into my loader cell as tank 1B started to pull us out of the killing zone, over the dune, to a hiding position.

It was already evening. Our force and other IDF units in the area had stopped the Egyptian attack. Barak Sunray ordered us to turn a few kilometers east to the makeshift base for a night's rest. The tanks needed essential maintenance and refueling; their ammunition supply needed to be restocked, and their weapon systems checked. We, their crews, needed a good night's sleep before returning to the battlefield at sunrise. We had to support the frontline until the reserves arrived.

1B slowly towed us behind the rest of Barak force and stopped at the technical support section of the base. I released the towing cables from 1B, who then went to the tanks' night parking.

The rest of the crew climbed down, and we stood in front of our tank.

"I will ask the technical team for immediate service," Tobi said and disappeared.

I walked around to check the base for showers and, hopefully, to find a kitchen facility.

The base had a few sections. The first was the medical area—a field hospital with a few Indian military tents for the medical staff and a couple of long military tents for injured soldiers. A small flat field designated as a helipad was marked at the corners with diesel-soaked rags burning in empty cans to light the landing spot at night.

Next to it was the technical support area with a few damaged tanks waiting for repairs, Reo trucks, APCs, cargo trucks, Reo crane trucks, and tents for spare parts.

The infantry and tank parking areas were in two lines. A bunker was next to their area, filled with shells and ammo boxes and organized by type.

A special area was designated for cleaning and maintenance. There were half-drums filled with a mixture of diesel fuel and oil, hundreds of 1-gallon cans with engine and transmission oil piled on the skids. and a diesel fuel truck.

Next I noticed the administration zone, supply tents, staff tents, Adjutancy, base commander and officers, and finally, at the corner, I found a big water tank with attached faucets and a few showerheads.

I walked back to our tank in the technical support area. "Any news?" I asked Ron and Guy. "Do you know when they will finish with the repairs?"

"Tobi said they would need to replace the engine and the drive sprocket, but they ran out of engines. Hopefully, they'll get one tomorrow," Ron answered. "He also said we needed to go to the Adjutancy and put our names on the list to be assigned to another tank. And to find an empty tent in the administration area and wait there until called."

We took our backpacks, the combat webbing equipment, sleeping bags, and foam mattresses and walked to the Adjutancy. One tent was marked Adjutancy with a black marker on white paper and attached to the canvas above the entrance.

"How can I help you, guys?" the sergeant asked as we entered the tent. He was sitting behind a large, wooden kitchen table. "Our tank is here for repairs, and we want to put our names on the list and get a tent for the night," Ron said.

The sergeant looked exhausted, dressed in a wrinkled, dusty work uniform; his three-stripes military rank was attached with a safety pin, barely hanging on to his sleeve. He looked at us with bloodshot eyes and handed me a clipboard with an attached form and a pen.

"Fill in this form, then go to the staff residence. The second tent from the back is empty. Inside, you'll find beds. If you're hungry, grab battle rations from the supply tent."

I looked at the clipboard. There were already a few completed pages, and the top one was ready to be filled out. We needed to submit our names, military service numbers, ranks, previous units, and a description of our duties. We finished it quickly as trained soldiers should.

The sergeant verified we had filled it in correctly and said, "I can see that we have a tank driver, a gunner, and a loader. We don't need drivers and gunners right now, but loaders and tank commanders are in high demand. I will call you when needed. Good luck." He looked at me.

"Thank you," I answered, and we walked away.

I knew that most casualties were loaders and tank commanders exposed to artillery and snipers. Pure ignorance and arrogance led us to fight the way we did, standing up with our upper body out of the turret instead of protecting ourselves inside the turret and using the periscopes designed for that purpose.

We found the tent the sergeant told us about. It was empty, with six dusty field beds covered with green foam mattresses. I put my stuff on one of the beds and went to lie down. My combat uniform had accrued another layer of dust and turned khaki-green from its original color of olive-green. I needed to remove my boots as my toes were itching. Three days had passed since I took them off. But first, I wanted to clean my uniform and bed from the dust. I took the mattress out of the tent and beat it by hand, raising a cloud of dust. I brushed my uniform, went back inside, sat on the bed, and removed my boots and socks. They were stiff, and the stench spread like a stink bomb. But I didn't feel anything except a sense of relief. I took my water bottle, washed my feet, and lay on the bed. It felt heavenly, like it was the softest bed I'd ever slept on.

"I'm going to bring food," Guy said, and I was glad. I didn't want to move from the bed.

CHAPTER 4

Break, October 8, 1973

Morning.

I visited our damaged tank to see the progress on repairs. The technical team had already worked on the tank and fixed the broken drive sprocket, but the engine replacement hadn't arrived yet.

Our mighty beast was lifeless, with a big hole in its guts.

Suddenly Tobi appeared at my side. "Hi, Amir, what tent are you?" he asked pleasantly.

"I'm with the crew at the second tent," I said. "Would you like to join us in our five-star meal with the best quality ingredients you can find, only in IDF Kosher battle-rations?"

He smiled and said he'd already eaten with the officers. Then he added, "Just know that we'll join our battalion as soon as the tank is ready."

"Yes, of course," I answered, wondering at the direction of his words.

"I don't want Ron or Guy to be part of my crew. I'm looking to replace them, but I'd like you to stay," he said.

I looked at him. "They are excellent soldiers and very professional," I said, disappointed. That was the last thing I wanted, to have Ron and Guy replaced with a new, unknown tank driver and gunner.

Toby didn't respond, and I nodded at him uncommittedly and walked back to the tent.

It was already warm outside, and inside the heat was stifling. Guy and Ron had folded the tent sides up to allow a little airflow.

Ron waved at me and asked, "Hey, what took you so long?"

"Oh, I met Tobi and had a chit-chat with him." I rolled my eyes. "You won't believe it, but this idiot wants a new crew for our tank and asked me to stay with him when it's ready." I threw my arms up. "This is terrible; I don't want a new crew, we have a strong bond, and he's unprofessional and ignorant. And…" Suddenly, I had that same gut feeling of absolute certainty about what would happen. "If he gets a tank to command, he will kill his crew!" I said in conviction.

Ron and Guy stared at me in silence.

I could only guess what was going through their minds.

God, help us. Let him find a different crew.

Guy broke the awkward moment and said, "Come try something. 'Chef' Ron fried the sardines in their tin on a small fire, and it's delicious." He handed me two sardines on a cracker.

To my surprise, it was tasty. "My compliments to the chef," I said to Ron laughing. Our mood changed and we ate the rest of the food, cans of corned beef, sweetcorn, and hummus. And for dessert, we shared a tin of sliced pineapple.

After eating, I sat on the bed and stared outside unfocused. Suddenly, I saw Mesika walking toward the central water truck. He was one of the cadets I had shared a room with during our tank commander training at Shivta.

What a great surprise! I rushed out, calling his name happily. "Mesika, Mesika."

He stopped and turned to me. He wasn't smiling. His eyes stared at me blankly, lifeless.

"Hey man, how are you? Where are all our friends? Do you have any news?" I bombarded him with my enthusiastic questions.

Mesika was quiet for a moment before he spilled out all that had happened in one long, tortured monologue.

"The first night was horrible. We thought we would easily join the outposts at the Bar-Lev line and keep the Egyptians from crossing the canal without confrontation or resistance. But when we approached the water, the Egyptian commandos and Armored Corps surprised us with missiles and RPGs. It was a massacre. Most of our tanks were destroyed by missiles. Some threw tracks and got stuck, and some sank in the sandy dunes, trapped and exposed in the battlefield fire zone. We never reached the Bar-Lev line…" He paused. His chest heaved with his heavy breathing.

"What about our friends?" I asked in a whisper. I needed to know, in spite of the sickening, gut-wrenching pain which his words brought upon me.

"Some were killed immediately by the missiles. Others, wounded, escaped the burning tanks only to be met by heavy artillery that soon finished them off. The few who survived retreated on foot back to our lines and were chased by commando squads. It was a nightmare. Some of our friends are missing, and most survivors who arrived here were sent to protect the northern Syrian border."

"What about Shaul?" I asked. He was my best friend at the Academy.

"Shaul is dead. So I heard. He was with three other crew members who survived Sagger attacks on their tanks. They carried one wounded on a stretcher and tried joining our forces. But the Egyptian commando tracked them down through their radio communications. They found a small concrete hideout, hoping to hold up until our troops could come to their rescue. Only, at that time, no one could go and save them. They fought back with their Uzis, which, as you know, are no match in power or range to the AK-47s the commandos use." Mesika stopped, and his eyes bored through me without seeing me, as if he were in a trance. His voice remained monotonous as he continued.

"They had no chance, none. Their only hope was that shelter. The injured soldier's condition worsened, and their water supply and ammo diminished rapidly. Their last radio transmission said that the Egyptians were firing artillery and antitank shells at them."

I listened in shock to his tale of horror. "How do you know that Shaul is dead? Maybe he escaped or was taken as a POW?"

Mesika looked at me with teary eyes. "An antitank missle hit the window where Shaul had taken his position. He was decapitated. The radio was on, and the other soldiers reported the situation live. In their last transmission, they desperately requested help. Then, the radio went silent. I don't know any more than that," Mesika said in a hushed tone, dropping his gaze.

I stood frozen. *Shaul, my friend, is dead! We talked, laughed, ate together, and shared the goodies he got from his Kibbutz only two days ago. How can it be? I will never hear his voice again, his brilliant ideas and intelligent solutions. In a split second, it was all over. He has lost his life, and the world has lost a bright young man who could have contributed much.*

Why?

Why him?

Is it just a coincidence? Him being in the wrong place at the wrong time?

Is our life so meaningless?

★★★

My parents, as Zionist-Socialists, had no room for God in their hearts. They raised me without any religious beliefs, which at that moment might have helped my inconsolable heart.

In a way, being Orthodox or a believer could provide justification, strength, and mental resilience in such extreme situations. Yet, the religious saying: "The LORD gave, and the LORD has taken away. Blessed be the name of the LORD," didn't carry any real value or deep meaning for me. It was just a cliché.

★★★

Mesika also told me that he had arrived at the base a day earlier. All loaders and commanders who had survived were immediately sent to the Golan Heights on the Syrian border to replace the wounded soldiers and the dead.

Mesika was a tank driver, and drivers weren't in urgent demand at the Syrian frontier. On the first night, he lost his tank when it sank to its belly in the sand and couldn't be towed as the cables had snapped. He and his crew managed to walk safely eastward and join our forces.

CHAPTER 5

New Crew, October 10, 1973

I woke up to a loud voice saying, "We're looking for a loader. Is anyone here a loader? We're ready to move right away."

I opened my eyes and saw a young, Armored Corps officer walking around our tents. He seemed to be in his twenties, tall and thin, with black hair and shiny bright black eyes. I noticed, looking out of the folded-up tent entrance, a tank parked near the medical section. *Had the reserve unit arrived to reinforce our forces?* I wondered.

The officer called again. "Any loaders here?"

I felt some excitement. "I'm a loader," I answered.

Any tank commander will be better than Tobi.

This was an excellent opportunity to find another one. I didn't want to leave Ron and Guy behind, but Tobi didn't want them back as his crewmen. We would probably be separated soon anyway, and I didn't wish to stay with Tobi!

The officer approached me. "Hey, soldier, do you want to join our crew? We're short of a loader," he said quietly.

"Sure, no problem," I said and started collecting my belongings. Ron and Guy looked at me with long faces.

"Bye, Amir, good luck," Guy said.

And Ron added, "Take care. See you after the war."

I left the tent and followed the officer.

"I'll take your backpack and sleeping bag," he said and grabbed my stuff, walking toward his tank. "You're overloaded." He smiled at his own pun. "My name is Shabtai, but you can call me Shabbi like everyone else."

Such a well-meaning name. Shabtai is the Hebrew name for Saturn, and I knew it to be the sixth planet from the Sun and the second-largest in our solar system.

"I'm Amir," I said. "But I can't call you Shabbi. You're an officer, and I'm still a cadet at the Tank Commander Academy."

"No problem," he laughed. "Maybe later, when you get to know me better."

We walked toward a tank marked with the number four, which meant he was the company deputy commander. We reached the tank. Two soldiers, probably the gunner and the driver, stood next to the tracks and looked at me curiously. They both seemed older than me, but to be honest, when you were nineteen years old, people in their mid or late twenties looked old to you.

One of the two, who looked somewhat somber, said, "Hi, I'm Ami, the driver."

"Hello, loader. Welcome to our team. My name is Yoav, and I'm the gunner," the other soldier introduced himself with a broad smile.

"Nice meeting you, guys. I'm Amir," I said with mixed emotions. They were older, with shared history and experiences. How would they accept me? How would I fit in? I missed my friends from the Academy, their jokes, their way of talking, their attitude, and their stories about girls. These guys might be family men, with jobs and kids even!

Shabtai said, "Amir will be our loader. He's a cadet at the Academy in active duty service. His tank was damaged by Sagger yesterday. Make him feel at home."

"Welcome aboard, Amir." Ami patted my shoulder before turning to enter his cell. And Yoav added, "Yeah, man, soon you'll feel like one of us," chuckling as he went up to his place under the commander hatch.

I climbed up to check the loader cell and organize my stuff. Standing on the track's mudguard, I saw the entrance to the hatch. It was covered with dried, dark red blood. My blood ran cold.

Oh, God! I can't stay here. This is a bad omen.

Shabtai watched me and said quietly, "Let's clean this first."

I was waiting to hear more details, but no one offered. I took the five-liter water jerrycan, shut the entrance lid, and poured water on the blood. Its color changed to bright red, as if it was coming alive again. It drained down from the top of the turret in tiny red streams as if it wanted to tell me what had happened.

It made me sick to my stomach. I was wiping and cleaning the blood with a dirty rag, feeling as if I was disrespecting the wounded loader. *Or dead?*

There must be a better way of doing this. But no other option came to my mind.

Shabtai helped me with the cleaning. "We must rush. Our company needs us as soon as possible," he said.

After a few more minutes, we were finished, and the part of the turret closest to the loader hatch was clean. As I entered my cell, I noticed there weren't any machine guns there.

"This is the loader," I said over the internal radio system. "We are missing two 0.3 machine guns."

Shabtai answered, "Yes, we know. We got the tank without them."

I glanced at him, surprised, but had nothing else to say. I stood on the loader chair with my torso above the turret to help with the navigation.

"Ami, drive back to our company," Shabtai ordered.

The tank's engine roared and started moving in a north-easterly direction.

We followed a few track prints on the desert ground when suddenly I saw a few tank-like shapes in the distance.

Shabtai looked through his binoculars and said, "They're ours. Ami, approach the tanks 1,500 meters on our right," he told the driver.

"Will do," Ami replied and turned the tank half-right. A few hundred meters away from the site, he stopped.

These tank-like shapes turned out to be burned and severely damaged Shot-Kal tanks. They looked lifeless. Like giant metal monsters who had lost their human patrons and now had no value. Just 50 tonnes of cold, dead steel. *What a depressing sight!*

We came closer to the first one, and Shabtai looked over from the turret. "We won't find anything here. Everything is burned. Let's check the others."

We moved to the next damaged tank. The turret had a small hole, probably a direct hit by a Sagger.

"Stop here, Ami. Let's see the condition of the machine guns. Amir, go check," Shabtai said.

I climbed out from the front of the tank and stood on the track mudguard. The smell inside was horrific, a mixture of burned flesh, melted steel, and copper. *Since the tank didn't blow up, maybe some of the crew survived.* I felt relieved by that thought.

I carefully entered the turret through the loader entrance, afraid I would find bodies inside, but it was clear. Then I looked at the co-axial machine gun. It seemed intact. I opened its top cover, unloaded the ammo belt, and pulled the charging handle twice to ensure it was empty of bullets and safe to handle. I was very proficient as a loader, knew the weapon systems and parts by heart, and assembled and disassembled machine guns very fast; I could even do it with my eyes closed.

The machine gun was in good working condition. I removed it from its base and handed it to Shabtai, who stood on top of the turret.

He took it and asked me to check the one mounted on the top of the turret at the side of the commander's hatch.

I tried to open the commander cell lid from 90 degrees to the horizontal position to have more room and easy access to the machine gun, but it didn't move. I entered the commander cell, stood on his chair, and checked if the machine gun was clear and safe to handle. It was fine and in operational condition.

Everything looked fine, but when I tried to remove the machine gun from its base, one of the pins was bent and stuck. I asked for a hammer and tried to knock it out. It was essential to get the machine gun out.

"We have to leave now; the company needs us immediately," Shabtai said.

"A few more seconds, sir. The first pin is already out," I said and hammered as hard as possible on the second pin to break the base. The machine gun was released from the turret, and though still attached to part of the base, it was useable. I handed it to Shabtai.

We took the two machine guns inside our tank. Shabtai checked the map, contacted the company commander to confirm their location, and directed Ami on the right course he'd need to take for us to join our forces. "Let's move," he said.

After a few more minutes, we saw heavy marks left by steel tank tracks that had scored and scratched the otherwise untouched miserable desert land. The terrain was rigid and flat, without vegetation, and we could drive fast.

I went down to my cell, inside the turret, to install the machine gun in its place parallel to the cannon. I then set up the firing mechanism, loaded it with ammo, and locked it in safe mode.

"The co-axial MG is ready to work," I said to the crew.

Shabtai said, "Okay, let's try it. Co-axial machine gun four hundred meters, at three o'clock, to the bush." He commanded, "Gunner, engage the main gun stabilizer."

"On target," Yoav said.

I pulled the charging handle, released it, loaded the first bullet in the chamber, and said, "Loader is ready."

"Fire at will," Shabtai ordered.

The machine gun started to fire approximately 500 rounds per minute at the target. Everything was working fine, and Shabtai praised us. "Great job, guys. We just killed an enemy bush," he said, and burst out laughing.

The tank galloped toward the company line of fire. Suddenly the radio came on.

"4, 4, this is Sunray. Over."

"This is 4; on my way to your location. Over," Shabtai answered.

"This is Sunray. Hurry up. We need all guns right now. Over."

"Wilco out," Shabtai said.

I felt the tension building up inside me. In the distance, I saw a hill of one-kilometer width, with 10 tanks in various positions. Some were at the hull-down, firing, and others at turret-down, watching the fire and suggesting corrections to the tanks shelling next to them.

It was executed by the book, exactly how we, the cadets, had practiced at the Academy.

Our line of defense was highly active. The hill looked like it was under an intense thunderstorm. We were surrounded by flashing lights, smoke rising from tank cannons and enemy artillery, and the loud sound of exploding shells.

"Be ready," Shabtai said. "In five minutes, we'll join our company. Our battle station is at the right side of the force; Ami, close the driver's lid and position the tank fifty meters to the right of 3B."

Ami closed the hatch and navigated the tank to the location that Shabtai ordered. He was very skilled and didn't need Shabtai to guide him step by step.

The crew members of commanders and their deputies were selected, mostly, according to their proficiency and expertise. So that the commanders and the deputies could deal with their additional tasks of strategies and operations.

Ami slowed down the tank when we approached the foothill.

"Move forward slowly to turret-down position, and…stop now," Shabtai commanded.

"Sunray, this is 4. Holding position right of 3B. Out to you." Shabtai reported to the company commander. "3B, this is 4, you can go to hull-down position. I'll watch your fire. Over."

3B moved a few meters ahead to the fire position.

Shabtai and I raised our bodies as high as possible until our torsos were above the turret. We both used our binoculars and looked around the killing zone in front of us. It was a large, 4,000-meter plateau, with many enemy tanks and armored personnel carriers on fire. About 1,500 meters in front of us, Egyptian tanks and infantry were attacking our front defense line, moving slowly toward us.

"3B, this is 4. 2,200 ahead enemy tank at one o'clock. Fire at will. I will watch your fire. Over," Shabtai said over the radio network.

"Wilco. Out," 3B answered.

I saw 3B advance to hull-down, aim, and shoot. A loud boom was heard, followed by a ball of fire from the cannon. A cloud of dust covered the tank. Shabtai and I both watched the trajectory of the shell. It was short, which meant it fell in front of the target.

Shabtai said, "Short."

3B fired again as soon as the dust cleared. The shell hit the ground behind the Egyptian tank.

"Long," Shabtai reported.

The third shot hit the target directly. A huge fireball followed by secondary explosions destroyed the enemy tank. I didn't notice any survivors jumping out.

"Good job, 3B. Watch my fire now," Shabtai said.

"Wilco," 3B answered, driving the tank back, and switching to turret-down to watch our fire.

Shabtai gave the sequence of fire commands. "Cannon, APDS, 2,500 meters, enemy tank."

I loaded the cannon with an APDS shell and said, "Loader is ready."

Yoav said, "Gunner is ready," and I knew he had set the range and switched to armor-piercing shells.

"Driver, go ahead slowly."

The tank climbed gradually to the hull-down position.

"On target," Yoav said.

"Stop," Shabtai said.

Ami stopped immediately as the tank reached the optimal hull-down height.

"Fire," ordered Shabtai.

The first shell left the cannon within five seconds with a loud blasting sound. The whole tank shook.

"Long and left," 3B reported.

I loaded the second shell, and Yoav released it when the dust cleared.

"Short," 3B said.

"Self-correction," said Yoav.

The third shell was on its way.

"Target," 3B confirmed.

Ami didn't wait. Every second in the hull-down position was dangerous to the tank and crew. He shifted to reverse and rolled back downhill and slightly to the right until Shabtai stopped him.

"4, 4. This is Braz Sunray. Stop firing at long range immediately. We're short on ammo. We have to wait until the enemy is close. We must hit each target with only one shell. Over," I heard the radio transmission from our company commander.

"This is 4. Wilco," Shabtai answered. He turned to me, "Amir, count the types and number of shells."

I checked the ammo and reported immediately, as requested. "We have five HEAT, five APDS, and seven HESH rounds."

Shabtai then called on the company radio frequency, "Braz stations, this is 4. Count your ammo and report directly. Over."

The answers came directly from each tank. We were short on our ammo, truly short, and the Egyptian offensive wasn't slowing down.

"Braz stations, this is 4. All tanks with more than two sets of rounds go back one hundred meters, unload the extra rounds, and return at once to your position. The process will be performed tank by tank. Platoon One will start, then Two, and last Three."

Tank by tank drove back and dropped the extra shells on a tarp laid on the sand behind the line. We were the last tank on the list. I prepared two HEAT, one APDS, and seven HESH. Ami drove to the location, stopped the tank, and jumped out to help unload the shells together with Shabtai. One by one, I handed the rounds to Shabtai, who gave them to Ami, who placed them on the tarp. It was quick, and we were done in under two minutes.

We drove back to our post, Shabtai stopped the tank at the turret-down position, and we observed the killing zone in front of us.

I felt anxious, truly awful.

How can we protect ourselves with such a low supply, with the enemy advancing and attacking us?

"Braz stations, this is 4," I heard Shabtai over the radio. "All tanks short of two sets of rounds drive back one hundred meters, load the shells needed, and return to your position. Go in the same sequence as before, Platoon One first, and one tank at a time. Over."

The first tank moved back and loaded the missing shells, and when all tanks had armed themselves, we stood in position, waiting for the Egyptian force to move forward.

Then it was clear to me. We couldn't afford to use any ammo on standard firing sets. We needed to shoot-to-kill at a short distance where the chances of hitting the target on the first shot were higher, though the risks of being shot at were highest.

"Braz stations, this is Sunray. Don't shoot targets above a range of 800 meters. Stay in turret-down position until they are close."

★★★

The killing zone was on fire. Tens of Egyptian tanks were smoking. Some exploded, their turrets separated from the hulls, looking like decapitated beasts. Some tanks were on fire, and others stood still and lifeless.

At the far end of the plateau, another wave of Egyptian tanks, APCs, and infantry, who marched behind the vehicles, advanced toward us in attack formation.

We were waiting. The tension grew higher, and adrenaline rushed through my body. No one spoke.

The enemy approached closer and closer, yet nobody was in a hurry to initiate that armageddon. Each side had understood that today, one of the forces would pay a heavy price, the ultimate sacrifice.

Shabtai turned to me. "Bring me one of your Uzi magazines," he said.

I took one and gave it to him. He removed the first bullet, put it inside my combat uniform's top pocket, and said quietly, "This is only for the worst-case scenario."

"This is Braz Sunray. Hold your fire. Out." The radio came alive.

The Egyptian army was still more than 3,000 meters away. Watching through the binoculars, I counted 30 tanks moving toward us. My heart beat fast.

Then the artillery shells started dropping around us. Their impact wasn't precise but forced us to stay low inside the turret. Mushrooms of smoke and dust rose in the air as the enemy tanks moved to a distance of about 2,000 meters.

We still waited.

"This is Braz Sunray. The enemy is now at a 1,000-meter range. Advance to hull-down position and fire at will. I repeat, fire at will. Out."

All 10 tanks simultaneously moved forward to fire position in a display of deadly power.

I jumped inside the turret, ready to act. It was so close. Too close. There wasn't time for tactics. The faster the gunner could shoot, the better our chances of survival.

"Amir, load APDS," Shabtai commanded. "Ami, go ahead a few meters. Yoav, APDS shoot at will. Three tanks ahead."

Yoav asked, "Which range?"

Shabtai answered, "It doesn't matter. They're too damn close. Aim and shoot."

"Stop now," Shabtai told Ami and turned the turret toward the first tank.

"I'm on target," Yoav said.

"Fire," Shabtai said.

Our tank released its first shell, and I heard the sound of a close strike immediately after the noise of the firing cannon.

Yoav shouted, "Target."

Shabtai aimed the cannon roughly toward the next tank. "The Egyptian tank is driving fast," he said.

I loaded the second APDS shell and announced, "Loaded."

Yoav said, "On."

"Fire," Shabtai ordered.

I heard Yoav's disappointment when we missed that one. Then, I loaded the last APDS shell. Yoav shot and hit the second tank.

"We're out of APDS," I announced.

"Prepare HESH," Shabtai commanded.

We had five of them, but they were slow speed and high ballistic curve, not the best ammo for this situation.

The combined firepower of 10 tanks shooting all at once was devastating. All around us were balls of fire, heavy smoke, and the terrible sound of explosions. The clouds of dust and smoke obscured our visibility, and Shabtai told Ami to return to the turret-down position until we could see better.

When the dust and smoke started clearing away, the sight was horrible, like a scene from Dante's inferno. Burning Egyptian tanks, wounded soldiers lying on the ground, screaming in pain, begging for help as the undamaged tanks retreated, leaving hundreds of infantry soldiers behind.

I looked through my binoculars in utter disbelief. The infantry forces continued to march toward our defense line.

"Gosh, it's not over yet!" I muttered. This was picked up by the internal radio, and Shabtai nodded in confirmation.

In a battle against infantry troops, shells were not considered as effective as machine guns, which were partially missing in our company. Our tank did have three working machine guns, though. One co-axial for the gunner's use, one for me, and one for the commander.

Shabtai ordered us to start using the machine guns in coordination with the other tanks. Ami drove the tank to the hull-down fire position. I loaded the co-axial for Yoav's use, jumped up to the loader machine gun for my use, and all three machine guns started to spit fire.

Yoav's was the most precise, and at the 500-meter range, the Egyptian soldiers were an easy target. There were hundreds of them, maybe even more. Some of them dropped when our bullets struck them, but those who weren't hit continued to walk forward slowly, without trying to hide or run for protection. They just marched on toward their deaths like they didn't care if they lived or died and were finished with their miserable tasks in this world.

I felt terrible. Horrified.

What the hell is this? Why don't they try to fight? Protect themselves? Or retreat, hide or surrender?

What's wrong with them?

I couldn't understand it. *They are people just like us. With families, kids, brothers, sisters, and friends. A life. What has made them give up on everything just like that? And for what?*

No sense of happiness or elation for our success in upholding the line filled my heart. At that moment, I wasn't able to think what would have happened to us if the Egyptians had won the battle.

The Egyptians had stopped the attack. The remaining forces retreated to re-group. And we didn't know if another wave of them was yet to come.

★★★

"What the fuck happened with the ammunition, Shabi?" Ami suddenly asked. "How come we're so short? How can we hold up the line if the army runs out of tank shells?" His voice was raised, and I shared in his emotion.

"The battalion deputy is dealing with it. He's already sent a few emergency transmissions to say we were out of ammo and won't be able to carry on," Shabtai answered calmly.

He was such a relaxed, calm and collected character, and I admired that.

"And..." Ami interjected impatiently.

"Our battalion got an order to hold the position at any cost. We can't leave this line and must stop the Egyptians here. We'll get the supply ASAP."

"What a response! Are we supposed to stand on top of the hill and throw stones at the Egyptian army?" Yoav asked.

"I'm positive it will arrive before the next offensive," Shabtai said before going silent.

Looking at him, I could see the stress in his face and the concern he didn't want to share with the crew.

Suddenly, I heard heavy engines and saw a few cargo trucks stopping about 200 meters behind us. They were bringing us the new supply of ammo. We were all relieved.

Shabtai immediately organized the loading sequence. He sent one tank at a time to load only five sets of shells, while the rest of the company kept the line at full alert, ready for any new attack.

We were the last to load. Ami drove the tank down the hill and stopped beside the trucks. He and Shabtai got out while Yoav stood on the mudguard, ready to take the shells from Ami. Shabtai handed them to me inside the turret.

I got the first box. It looked somewhat different in color and design. Even though the shape and size were the same as what we normally used, the cartridges were silver, not copper, and the color of the heads was different. All captions were in English. "What are these ammunitions? They look strange," I asked Shabtai.

"Looks American," he said.

That was a surprise. I didn't have time to ponder this information, but I felt very uncomfortable. How could it be that our emergency supply was so depleted after only three days of war that we needed the Americans to restock us with essential tank ammunition? I shook my head in dismay.

"Lucky that the U. S. is on our side," I responded.

I checked the lot number and organized the shells by sets, then placed them at a standby position on the floor within easy reach. Once I got more ammo boxes, I'd put them in the designated storage underneath the removable bottom.

"Done. Everything is in order," I said to Shabtai.

"Good. Let's return to our post," he said.

We entered our cells and prepared for the drive back. It took us less than a minute to get back to the foothill next to 3B, still at turret-down position, watching for any suspicious movement.

I looked through my binoculars at the "Valley of Death," my nickname for the battlefield. Burned tanks and APCs were scattered all around. Some were still smoking. The bodies of the Egyptian soldiers were left behind on the sand where they had fallen. The smoke climbed straight up to the sky in a long cylindrical shape, so straight and perfect, without any deformation…like it was touching God. I'd never seen anything like that before. Nothing was alive there. Humans and machines were all dead. A flock of black vultures circled above the valley, eyeing and hissing at the sights of death.

★★★

It was already afternoon. The company's tanks turned off their engines to save on fuel, and a sudden thick silence descended upon us. Some soldiers felt safe enough to climb down from their tanks. Small groups gathered to talk about the battle, the number of tanks destroyed, and the skillful tactics of our commander, who had ended the attack with the last shells in our possession. And most importantly, without any casualties on our side.

I stood aside. I didn't know anyone in the company except for my tank team. Most were older than me. Long-haired reserve soldiers who had served together since their active duty days. They chatted about the jobs they had left behind being called to service on such short notice. Businesses they'd run and their worries about meeting commitments. Some men were married with kids and shared pictures of newborn babies and their young, beautiful wives left at home, with goodbye kisses and a promise to return soon.

Being nineteen years old and on active duty, I had nothing in common with them. My unit, which I was now separated from, had suffered a massive loss in the first two days of the war. My brothers-in-arms were lost to me. Now I was amongst strangers.

I went back into the tank, cleaned the loader cell, took the cannon shells and empty machine gun cartridges, and threw them outside. Keeping them inside was a risk. They could be caught in the gear of the turret and the tank hull and damage the mechanism that allowed 360 degree rotation. Or, they might cause an electrical shortage to the batteries on the floor, start a fire, or make the electrical systems malfunction.

Shabtai received a message on the radio. He told us to get ready to move to a gathering point to make camp at sunset, where we'd fuel, load more ammo, maintain the machine guns, and get fresh water in the jerrycans. In other words, prepare the tank for the next day of battle.

We traveled east to the designated parking area, which was well-organized so we could quickly finish all the essential maintenance for the next day's assignments. Ami checked the engine's oil levels and transmission, inspected the tracks and drive sprockets, and filled the tank with fuel. Yoav cleaned and oiled the main gun, and I cleaned the machine guns and checked their calibration and functionality. Our last task was carrying the heavy ammo boxes from the bunker and filling up all the empty storage inside the tank.

Shabtai fussed over us like a mother hen, offered his help to all of us, and then left for the officers' briefing. By the time we had completed all the chores and eaten our battle rations it was already past 10:00 p.m. It had been a long day, and I needed a good night's rest. Most of the crews had already gone to sleep, but I wanted to clean up first. My face and hair were covered with layers of dust, oil, and ash, and I felt sticky and dirty. I tried to wash the grime off with a 10-liter jerrycan full of water, but it did little. So, I looked for the heavy-duty soap bar we used to wash dishes with and lathered my head, scraping my scalp hard. It did the job well, and next, I washed my hands and brushed my teeth. Only then did I feel clean enough to go to sleep.

At first, I considered sleeping on the sand close to the tank tracks, which would be the most comfortable place. But then I decided against it. The best protection from scorpions and other unfriendly desert creatures would be lying on top of the tank.

I unpacked my sponge mattress, laid it on the engine and transmission protective plates, placed my sleeping bag on the mat, and removed my boots. *Ah, that feels so good.*

We would leave before dawn tomorrow morning, which gave me about seven hours of sleep. That was a real treat. Rarely had I enjoyed a whole night of sleep without any guard duty since the beginning of my military service. *What a luxury!*

CHAPTER 6

Can it Be? October 10–13, 1973

The guard on duty shouted, "Five o'clock, wake up! Wake up and get ready to leave the camp before sunrise. At five-thirty your company will start moving."

Thirty minutes to get ready was hardly enough time for me. Without delay, I jumped out of the sleeping bag and put on my Nomex overall, the special flame resistant overall designed mainly for tank crew. A heavy-duty ribbon hidden under a zipper at the back of the Nomex could be used to pull wounded soldiers out of the tank.

I looked at my watch to check the time. It was a fancy, automatic Seiko Bell-Matic with a sapphire blue dial and a silver-toned stainless steel bracelet, luminescent hands and markers, day and date display, and was water-resistant up to 100 meters; an expensive gift my parents had given me when I started my military service. I used its alarm system to wake me up early so I could manage my time properly.

I washed my face and put on my socks and boots. That was the lengthiest task at hand. I rolled up two rubberbands on top of my socks, just above the top end of my boots, and folded the bottom edges of my pants, around the hidden rubberbands to straighten and tighten my pants.. Now, I felt like a real soldier. These reserves looked like homeless people, with their long, dusty, messy hair and unshaven stubble. Wearing mismatched uniforms, their shirts hung down over ill-fitting pants that covered their boots and swept the ground.

Ami walked out. He was dressed and ready in five minutes. Yoav was the next to finish. I hadn't seen Shabtai around and presumed he was in the officers' briefing. A few minutes later, he arrived.

"Hey, guys," he said in a cheerful tone. "Are you ready?"

"Sure," Yoav said. "I marked four Xs yesterday and am ready to add more." Yoav engraved an X on the side of the cannon guardrail for each tank he destroyed.

I stared at him, uncomfortable with his actions. It seemed to me he tried to lessen the gravity of the war, and I turned my gaze away. But, in fact, what Yoav did was quite understandable. A gunner saw the target through the periscope for a few seconds at a time before aiming and shooting. The faster he fired, the better a gunner he was. And Yoav was an excellent one.

Also, since the tank—when not shooting—was positioned in turret-down behind a landscape obstacle, the gunner didn't get the same full view of the battle zone as the commander and the loader. In a way, the gunner was spared the horror.

My attitude was more somber than Yoav's.

"Amir?" Shabtai looked at me.

"Everything is ready," I answered. "We loaded the ammo last night. The machine guns are loaded and ready to use, the main gun is cleaned and oiled, and all weapon systems are checked and working."

"We fueled the tank to the maximum yesterday," Ami said. "Checked the oil level and added a little, the transmission oil level is fine, and the tracks' tension is good to go."

Ami, like Yoav, wasn't exposed to the vistas of the battlefield. The driver sat at the tank's lowest point and didn't see the actual fighting directly, even at a hull-down position when the tank was shooting. Both Yoav and Ami learned the details of battle mainly from internal radio communications.

"Great teamwork," Shabtai said. "Sorry I couldn't help you as much as I wanted to, but I had plenty of administrative duties to deal with." He shrugged apologetically. "We got several radio communications regarding coordination with the support technician group. I had to push the supply of food, water, fuel, and ammo and also sent the list of the crews in our company to Adjutancy for follow-up." He paused and asked again, "So, are we ready to move?"

"Yes, we are ready," we answered in tandem.

"So, what do you have for us today?" Ami asked.

"We have to hold a defense line fifteen kilometers northwest of here," Shabtai said. "We got intelligence that the Egyptians will try to break through this area. Our battalion will take the position there and establish the defense line before sunrise."

We entered the tank, each going to his cell, ready to move. It was 5:30 a.m.

In the east, the sky started to glow in reddish, orange, and golden hues. Dawn slowly crawled up from the corners of the dark night and overtook the brightness of the stars. Our lined-up tanks, standing on the arid, forsaken land, had slowly emerged out of the shadows.

★★★

"Braz stations, this is Braz Sunray. Be ready to move on my command. Over."

All the tanks turned their engines on, disturbing the desert silence with the noise of their rumbling. Company by company, the tanks moved out, following the battalion commander to our destination. A few kilometers away from our endpoint, the commander stopped the convoy.

"Bamba, this is Braz Sunray. Proceed forward, check and confirm the area is safe from a potential ambush by the commandos. Over," he ordered the armored infantry recon patrol unit, code-named 'Bamba.'

"This is Bamba, confirmed. The area is clear. Over."

"This is Braz Sunray. Take positions at the two far sides of our force."

The main job of the recon unit, Bamba was to alert the tanks to incoming missiles. They split into two groups and took positions at the far ends.

The battalion started moving forward again.

I noticed a few long dunes in front of us in the distance.

"Braz stations, this is Sunray. Follow me and position yourselves at a turret-down along the hill according to our standard battle formation. 1 and 2 on my left, 3 and 4 on my right. Out." I heard our battalion commander over the radio. Then, each company moved to its designated battle position behind a long foothill in the dunes in a turret-down position.

We turned off the engines and operated all electronic and power systems with the tanks' batteries.

The sun started to rise. At first, only a red hairline of light appeared, making the sky more radiant than ever. Then the sun climbed higher and higher until it felt as if a massive fireball had appeared above our heads. It was heating the desert up from the cold of night, fast.

★★★

Shabtai and I stood on our chairs, watching the plateau ahead. It was quiet. No movement. I took my binoculars and looked again. Just a dreary wilderness with a few acacia trees, some bushes, and the skeletons of deserted cars. Nothing much to see.

The company commander ordered us to leave a single tank from each platoon at a turret-down position to watch for and warn of any potential danger. The rest of our company tanks, including ours, moved back and stayed in a full hiding position. I felt relaxed; nothing was going on at that moment, and we decided to have breakfast.

Shabtai called Yoav and asked for my binoculars. Yoav jumped out of the turret, and they both crawled to the top of the dune. They checked the area using binoculars and built a range map by estimating the distance to the objects sticking out in the plateau in front of them: the future killing zone. Shabtai made a written list for himself and Yoav, indicated the following:

The tree at 12 o'clock = 3,000 meters.

The car skeleton on the trail at 11 o'clock = 2,500 meters

The group of three bushes at 1 o'clock = 1,200 meters

The big, black rock at 12 o'clock = 1,000 meters

The empty drum at 3 o'clock = 800 meters.

It was a significant advantage for the gunner and the commander to prepare a range map. It could speed up the time of the first shooting and minimize the number of shells needed to hit the target in a fire sequence.

"I have a surprise meal for you, guys," Ami said.

I raised my brows at him and asked, "How can a battle ration meal be a surprise?"

And Yoav retorted without even glancing over at me, "Our specials for today are: one can of corned beef, one can of hummus, one can of sweetcorn, one can of pineapple, and crackers on the side."

"What a shock. Don't we have sardines today?" Ami asked and laughed.

"Oh, yeah," Yoav said, "I forgot to mention it. Do you miss it?" He had a broad grin on his face.

Ami climbed on top of the armor grille plates that protected the engine and opened one of them with a rug. It was hot from the two massive exhaust pipes and the engine underneath. He then pulled out two tins of goulash we had received in some of the battle rations. They were well-heated, and I was surprised they didn't explode. But looking closely, I noticed two small holes on top of each tin to release steam.

"Hahaha," Ami, noticing me looking, burst out in loud, hearty laughter. "You can learn some tricks from your elders."

I smiled back. "Okay, you're right, but how does it taste? That's the question."

Ami opened the steaming goulash cans, took a fork, and lifted a piece of meat with it, "Here, try it," he said.

I blew on it to cool it down. It smelled appetizing, and my mouth watered. I took a bite and...*Oh my God!* It melted in my mouth and tasted heavenly, like home cooking. My home cooking.

Every Friday night, at 7:00 p.m., my family used to go to the Sabbath dinner in the central dining room in our village. My father, my little brother, and I would wash and dress in clean white shirts before waiting by the door for my mother's final inspection and approval. Then we would walk uphill along a narrow lane running between two lines of olive trees until we reached the big modern dining room. We sat around long, rectangular tables covered with white linen tablecloths and decorated with vases of flowers and greenery from the village greenhouse. The high-school kids led the Friday evening ceremony and sang traditional and modern songs for Sabbath. After that, they would serve us dinner.

Peretz, the cook, who'd immigrated from Hungary, prepared a special menu on Friday nights, which always included the traditional dish of Cholent. This was a Jewish Sabbath beef stew made with meat, bones, beans, and potatoes, and slow-cooked for hours until the meat fell off the bone. It was deliciously divine, and I loved it very much.

Ahh, I miss you guys. My family, my village, my home. Everyone and everything, I thought as the taste of the goulash brough back memories.

Ami put the two goulash tins on the mudguard. We opened other cans of food from the battle rations and started eating. We were hungry. Suddenly, out of the wilderness, a place without any sign of life, a cloud of flies swarmed over us to take their cut. They buzzed around the open cans, over our heads, grabbed at our food, and annoyed us. Eating quickly became a challenging task, with us waving our arms to scare them away and inspecting every bite carefully so as not to swallow bugs along with our food. I moved a couple of empty tins to the far side, hoping to attract them to that location, away from us.

Around 11:00 a.m., we got a radio transmission. "This is Sunray. All crews return immediately to your tanks and wait for further instructions. Out."

We quickly got up and climbed back into the tank, waiting. Soon after, we heard the radio again.

"This is Braz Sunray. There is movement about 5,000 meters west of us. Wait for my command to fire. Out."

Five kilometers was too far away. Our best performances were at around 3,000 meters or closer. Of course, we could shoot beyond that range, but the chances of hitting the target on the first attempt were slim. As a result, it would force us to use more ammunition and be exposed to the enemy for longer.

We operated our tanks better than the Egyptians. We were faster and better trained. Waiting for the enemy in a defensive line gave us a significant advantage. Yet, I had no idea how massive the attack would be or how many tanks were involved.

Will the commandos use their Sagger missiles? That was the most significant worry on my mind.

I felt the urgency of the situation in the air. I folded my loader chair and stood on the steel floor to check the shells and the co-axial machine gun once more. Everything was in order. I opened my chair and stood on top of it, side by side with Shabtai.

Another communication was heard on the radio. "This is Braz Sunray. Advance your tanks to turret-down position and observe the plateau ahead. Wait until the forces move closer, about 3,000 meters, which is next to the single tree in front of us. Fire on my command. Work in pairs as per usual."

I knew this drill by heart. We'd practiced it hundreds of times at the Academy. One tank would be at hull-down in firing position, and the other at turret-down to watch the strike and correct as needed. Hearing the commander's orders, though he didn't specify the steps, gave me the impression that these reserves knew what to do. They were experienced teams in Armored Corps.

"3B, this is 4; I will go first. Over," Shabtai radioed to the tank on our left, which stood 50 meters away.

"Wilco," the commander of 3B answered.

I watched the plateau in front of us and saw about twenty tanks moving in our direction. *Not so bad. The question is, how many are there behind them?*

The radio came on. "Enemy tanks are at 3,000-meter range. Fire at will."

Shabtai said, "3B, watch my fire." Then he gave the pre-fire sequence of commands while the tank was still at the turret-down position and not exposed to enemy fire. When Yoav and I confirmed we were ready, the tank climbed slowly to the hull-down position until Yoav said, "On target." Then the tank stopped at Shabtai's command, and his "Fire!" order came at once.

Yoav was very fast, and within five seconds, he'd aimed the periscope reticle to the center of the enemy tank and released the first shell toward the target. The loud sound of the cannon firing was deafening, but we never used earplugs as it wasn't considered masculine enough.

Without a wind to disperse the dust quickly, we couldn't see the target after firing. That was the job of the partner tank, and it followed immediately.

"4, this is 3B. Short and two left."

That meant that the shell had hit the ground short and to the right of the target. I immediately loaded the second APDS shell and said, "Loader is ready."

Yoav aimed again according to the correction, announced, "Fire," and released the second shell.

Yoav must have seen a bright flash by the targeted tank, even through the dust, as I heard him call, "Target."

3B confirmed. "It is a target."

Ami didn't wait. He shifted to reverse, and when Shabtai said, "Back and left," he drove the tank immediately to a concealed position. Then Shabtai ordered him to go ahead and right to turret-down, to watch 3B's fire sequence.

Shabtai and I stood high above the turret and watched the plateau through the binoculars. A few Egyptian tanks had been hit already and were either on fire or heavily damaged, with burned parts thrown around.

"Four, this is 3B; I'm ready to start. The target is at 11 o'clock. APC."

"This is 4. I'm ready."

I looked and saw the APC at a range of approximately 2,000 meters. 3B climbed to a hull-down position and shot a set of HEAT shells. We corrected their shots, guiding them to the target with a series of three rounds. The Egyptians responded with an artillery barrage, but it wasn't precise. We went back inside the turret, closed the lids, and waited for the fire to ease. One of our tanks had taken a direct hit to its transmission and needed towing.

Our advantage over the attacking Egyptian forces was clear. We hadn't suffered any casualties, had held our line of defense, and shot at long-range skillfully and efficiently.

At last, after two hours of that lethal dance, the offensive stopped. The Egyptian forces retreated and left behind about thirty damaged tanks, a few APCs, and thrown tracks.

Yoav announced he had added three more Xs to his list of hits. He was very proud of his achievements, and for a good reason; he was an outstanding gunner.

We waited until sunset and moved back to a secure night camp. It was already 7:00 p.m. by the time the company tanks parked up.

I started with the dirty job of cleaning and oiling the machine guns and the cannon's breechloader, calibrating them and testing their functionality. Then, I removed all empty bullet and cartridge shells from the turret.

I washed my face and hands and carried ammunition to fill up all the empty storage bins. On the battlefield, we had used twenty shells and five boxes of 0.3" bullets on belts.

Yoav and Ami were busy with their tasks. I asked for Yoav's help with moving 10 wooden boxes of 105mm shells for the cannon and we left them on the sand near our tank. After that, Yoav went to complete his duties.

I opened each box and verified all the shells had the same serial number. Then, I picked up three shells, one at a time, and loaded them on top of the mudguard at the front of the tank above the track. I climbed on the mudguard and lifted and placed each shell on top of the turret near the loader entrance. Then, I went up the turret, entered the loader cell, and moved the shells one by one into their secured storage area. Before I could finish, I needed to repeat the process six more times.

After putting the 18 shells and the machine gun ammunition boxes in their place, I felt exhausted. I thought it would be faster if I climbed from the mudguard to the top of the turret, holding one shell in my arms and placing it carefully near the loader hatch. I lifted the first of the shells from the last set and put it on the mudguard. It was an APDS. One arm held it at the base, and the other hugged its explosive head. This type wasn't the heaviest of the shells; they weighed about 20 kilograms each.

I held the shell tightly and started to climb on top of the turret. But when I bent to place it down, I suddenly lost balance. I panicked. If I let the shell hit the ground with its head, it would explode. I hugged its body tightly, protecting its head as I dropped down from the top of the tank's turret.

BOOM!!! I heard the massive explosion as it tore my body apart.

★★★

A peaceful sense of awareness spread over me. I felt complete. Perfect. Pure. Without any blemish. My senses had disappeared. I couldn't see, hear, or smell, or feel any emotion. My physical existence was left behind, and the laws of physics, which all the matter in the universe obeyed to, didn't apply to me anymore. I was weightless, without gravity, boundaries, or the limitations of time, mass, or any known energy.

I started to rise above the earth, floating without effort, calmly. Nothing bothered me anymore, not the war, not my friends, family, or country. It was not important. Life in this world seemed insignificant. The aches and pains we experience, the fears, the loves, desires, all that we achieve, and all that we want to gain or are afraid to lose. None of this mattered anymore.

The lives we live felt like a tiny fraction of our true existence, like something we must experience for a limited time to move on to the next meaningful state of being. All living beings must go through the physical life passage to reach completion.

A complete sense of peacefulness had arisen in me. I saw a bright, calming light that welcomed me from above. I floated upward to reach it.

Suddenly, a tiny thread of connection, a human emotion, woke up in my heart.

I must say goodbye to Mom. Just to tell her everything is okay. I sensed her presence. So far and yet so close. She pulled me back.

A powerful entity interrupted my ascension with an unarguable message: IT IS NOT YOUR TIME YET!

It wasn't up for discussion, and I felt I was descending back to reality.

★★★

I opened my eyes. I was sitting on the ground near the tank's track, holding the shell tightly with both hands. A sharp pain spread from my chin to my head. Did I have a concussion?

Was this for real? Had time stopped or slowed down until I returned?

It felt real to me!

It really happened to me.

Why wasn't it my time yet? What do I need to finish? Is it something to do with me? Maybe future generations?

I tried to stand up, but the ground was swaying in front of my eyes. I was dizzy, so I continued to sit on the yellow sand, with the shell resting against my thighs and my arms securing it tightly. It was intact. After a few more seconds, I lowered the APDS shell to the ground and held the tank track for support to get up. My jaw and head were screaming in pain, and I could hardly open my mouth. Nobody was nearby.

"Do you need help?" I suddenly heard Yoav's voice. He offered me his arm and pulled me to my legs. "Go up to the loader cell, and I'll pass you the shells," he said.

I sluggishly dragged my feet up the turret. I was still dizzy and worn out.

Yoav looked at me and asked, "Are you okay?"

I nodded and strained to answer. My whole face, from my jawline to my lips, eyes, and skin, ached. "Yes," I croaked.

"Good, then," Yoav said, and handed me the last two shells. I placed them in their designated locations and plummeted down onto my chair.

CHAPTER 7

POW, October 11, 1973

I opened my eyes. My head was still in pain, my jaw was swollen, and I could hardly speak. Even swallowing my saliva was painful.

Yoav entered the gunner's cell. Seeing me sitting at the loader chair with my battle uniform and boots, he said, "Amir, you woke up early today. First to be ready." He grinned and gave me a thumbs-up.

I slowly nodded my head. I didn't want him to know that this was how he'd left me the night before.

"Ah, stop acting like a crybaby. What happened is my fault. I shouldn't have walked on the turret with the heavy shell in my hands. Better not tell anyone.

Shabtai entered his cell and asked, "Are we ready? We'll move shortly."

Yoav was heard on the communication first. "Yes, I'm ready. Let's rock 'n' roll!"

"Ready to go," Ami immediately confirmed.

I struggled to open my mouth to say, "Yes" or "Loader is ready." It felt like I'd had multiple root-canal treatments at the dentist and my lips and tongue were still frozen. Finally, I managed to say, "Yes."

Tank engines started to roar, awakening the desert from its peaceful, deep repose.

"Ami, follow 3B and keep a 100-meter distance," Shabtai said.

Tank after tank proceeded forward, following the lead tank of the company commander. The three platoons drove in consecutive order; our tank, 4, was the last of the lot and closed the convoy, which left a massive cloud of dust behind it.

After driving for an hour, we arrived at a road where I saw an unorganized, makeshift camp of a few tents. They were small units of technical support, medics, and administration.

The soldiers were thrilled to see us, welcoming us with cheers and shouts, "You are the first to arrive for our protection."

We turned 2 kilometers west and stopped to establish our new line of defense. We found an appropriate standpoint and spread the tanks out in the standard battle formation, as before.

Ami positioned our tank at the far right, next to 3B.

I was still in pain, unable to eat anything, and struggled to drink water from the canteen, but I felt a little better. My jaw was hot and swollen, but it was hidden under my combat helmet with its communication headset and mouthpiece.

Most of the tanks were in a hide position, some in turret-down, watching to detect any movement from the west. Around 11:00 a.m., we got a radio transmission to be ready for the Egyptian armored forces that had been spotted advancing toward us. Bamba detected the enemy. They took a higher ground position at the two far sides of our battalion.

Our company commander radioed immediately: "Braz stations, this is Sunray. Place yourself in standard battle positions. Fire only on my command. Out."

And like a well-oiled machine, every other tank placed itself at a turret-down post while the others went into hiding mode.

Shabtai flagged 3B to stay at a hide position and told Ami to go slowly ahead until he stopped him at the turret-down location.

Both Shabtai and I looked for any sign of the approaching enemy, like dust or smoke from moving armored vehicles or tanks, but I couldn't see anything.

Suddenly, like dozens of kettles whistling all at once, a piercing noise cut through the air, followed by the blasting sound of explosions that shook the ground underneath us. Our tanks were covered with black smoke, dust, and sand.

That immediately brought back memories of the Six-Day War in 1967, when I was thirteen.

★★★

I had taken cover at a tiny shelter adjacent to my house. The Jordanians bombed our hamlet, targeting Israel's central propane and fuel storage reservoirs that were near the west side corner of our village. They used American Long-Tom cannons but had missed the fuel ranch reservoirs by a few hundred meters and instead shelled our houses.

The ground around the dark, crowded shelter shook and swayed after each massive explosion, and the sound was horrific. I was afraid the hiding place wouldn't hold up. There were only children and women left, as the men had been called for duty. Everyone was scared, but no one talked about it out loud. The expectation was that you show a brave face. That was the minimum contribution that the home front could make to the courageous soldiers fighting on all three frontiers—Egypt, Jordan, and Syria.

The siren screamed with the single-pitch, unpleasant wailing of the all-clear sound.

"Finally, it's over. Thank God!" our next-door neighbor said.

My mother took my five-year-old brother's hand and said, "It's time to go home. The bombing is over." We climbed a few stairs, opened the heavy iron door, and walked out of the public shelter with all the other families.

The night was very dark. A distant crescent moon looked down on us and did little to illuminate our village under blackout regulations. We walked as fast as possible to get home, but the 100-meter distance to our house felt like a long stretch. The olive trees on both sides of the lane swayed their heavy branches in the blowing wind, making scary crackling and rustling sounds.

Finally, we reached home. My mother lit candles as the power had been cut off. Long shadows danced on the walls from the movement of the small flames, and our house looked eerie and unnerving. A shudder went down my spine.

Suddenly an emergency alarm went off, tearing the silence apart. The bell, mounted on the front door, rang loudly. It was connected to the primary village incubator, holding thousands of goose eggs, which meant the temperature in the incubator had dropped below the minimum level. A risk to the life of the goose embryos inside. My father was normally responsible for the incubators, but he had been called to the army.

My mother looked at me. "Amir, you need to go now and check the situation," she said with a worried expression.

No one but me knew how to operate the emergency generator for the incubator and save the goose embryos.

I must do it! And now. I'm thirteen years old, a grownup. A few months ago, I had my Bar-Mitzva. After a brief ceremony at the synagogue, I had turned from a young boy into an adult with responsibilities and duties. *I'm not a baby anymore and must behave accordingly.*

I took the set of keys for the incubator room and the gate of the emergency generator, and a flashlight. "Don't worry, mom, I can fix the issue easily," I said before walking out to the road leading to the incubator.

The village was dark and silent. All the residents were in their homes. Walking downhill on the empty, spooky road, I heard a baby crying from a neighboring house. Large carob trees with dense, menacing canopies shaded me on both sides of the narrow trail, preventing the small moon far above from lighting my way. I started running, holding the keys and the flashlight tightly.

The temperature inside the incubator was already critically low, below 27 degrees Celsius. The lock of the iron gate of the generator room was jammed, and I needed to give it a rough shake before it would release. Finally, the gate opened wide with a noisy squeak. I had to go in and turn the generator on manually. I opened the electrical panel lid on the front of the generator, flipped up the heavy steel wings on each side to cool down its engine, and used steel rods to keep them open.

I turned on the main switch. A small bulb illuminated the control panel. I pushed the green "Start" button, but it didn't start the generator. I tried again but with no success. I knew that, like a car's engine, I could only try so many times before the battery would drain.

Panic raised my pulse rate as thoughts about losing all the goose embryos ran through my mind. *This will all be my fault! What a disaster.*

All I wanted was to run home, back to safety.

No! That would be wrong. I must stay, find the problem, and fix it. Dad always took care of the generator and set it in such a way that the green start-up bottom would work immediately after one push.

My brain started to analyze the situation. *What could have gone wrong? The start-up button is turning the starter motor but not igniting it? Maybe there is no gas.* I looked around the shed and found four, full 20-liter cans of diesel at the corner. I opened the generator tank, picked one of the heavy containers, filled it up, and pushed the green button again. Suddenly, the machine coughed, released smoke, and started working!

Relief spread through my body. The feeling was intoxicating. A sense of satisfaction and some pride replaced my fear of the bombs and the darkness. I checked that the incubator was working well, locked all the doors, and ran home light on my feet.

I was impatient to tell my mother about my success and how I had solved the problem of saving the eggs in the incubator. "Amir! What happened? Why did it take you so long? I was so worried," my mom said as I stepped inside.

And I'd told her proudly what had happened and how well I'd assessed the situation and restarted the generator. Exactly how she'd have expected me to do.

The same as now! In this war.

★★★

We ducked down inside the turret. Shabtai sat on his chair, only the top of his head, and his eyes peeking out of the turret as he signaled me to stay inside. The tank and its crew, sitting inside, were protected from artillery so long as the tank wasn't hit directly.

The sickening whistling sounds followed by the barrage of explosions continued.

"It's only a matter of time before the tanks and armored vehicles attack. They want to force us to keep our heads down," Shabtai said.

Then our company commander said on the radio, "Stay low and watch the area."

The artillery continued. One of our tanks took a direct hit to the engine compartment and burst into flames; its commander was injured, and the tank was out of action.

How could they know where we are? Our tanks are in turret-down positions, which are almost impossible to detect. Yet, they are firing at us with such precision. Unbelievable!

We held our position when we got the following radio transmission: "Braz stations, this is Braz Sunray. Four thousand meters ahead, the enemy is moving toward us. Set your targets by standard priority, and fire at will. I repeat, fire at will. Out."

Once again, our lethal dance had begun. Though this time, it was slower. The dust, smoke, and explosions of the artillery affected our ability to shoot fast and accurately. We had to stay longer in a hull-down position and be exposed to enemy fire to strike our targets.

The battalion started to lose tanks. At that stage, we'd already lost four. Some crews needed immediate evacuation. Holding the line was pricy, but the order was clear: keep the position. Retreat was not an option.

Our tank watched over 3B as it shot at the enemy. Using the binoculars, I observed the first shell. It hit the ground behind the target and I told Shabtai, who corrected the fire instruction to 3B. We did it three more times until 3B hit its mark.

The battlefield was filled with dozens of Egyptian tanks which had caught fire.

Suddenly, the Egyptian forces turned to the south in an organized and coordinated manner and began to disappear. The artillery gradually stopped too, and our line of defense went silent. There was no attack, no movement. It was unexpected, and we all thought the Egyptians were reorganizing to return for a new assault. Again, we put a few of our tanks in a turret-down position and the rest in a hiding position, watching the killing zone and expecting a renewal of the attack.

Nothing happened until unexpectedly I heard Shabtai say, "Look in the three o'clock direction. Do you see anything?"

I raised my binoculars and looked. "No," I answered.

"Look again. A lone soldier is walking toward us."

I checked again. "Yes. Now I can see," I said. "He hardly walks in these sandy dunes."

"He must be exhausted," Shabtai answered. "I'll call Bamba to pick him up."

We waited, but no one tried to approach the soldier. Shabtai called our company commander and got permission to pick up the Egyptian as a prisoner of war.

Ami started the engine, and the tank slid down the hill in the Egyptian soldier's direction. The soldier lifted his hands in surrender when he saw our tank approaching him.

I looked at his uniform and realized he was an officer. Shabtai asked me to cover for him, and I loaded the machine gun, ready to fire.

Shabtai jumped down from the tank, stood in front of the Egyptian officer, and spoke to him in Arabic. The officer placed his hands on the front of the tank as Shabtai searched his body for hidden weapons. He found a handgun that seemed to be a Beretta 9mm. He checked to see if it was loaded and then put it in his back pocket. Facing the Egyptian, he started to talk with him again. Shabtai seemed to be fluent in Arabic.

After a short conversation, he ordered the Egyptian to climb up to the turret. The officer sat down below my hatch, in front of us, facing forward and holding his hands behind his back.

It was the first time I had seen the enemy up close and personal. The man was a nervous wreck, exhausted and fearful. His facial expressions changed from despair to discouragement and misery; he must have been without hope after his people left him behind to the mercy of his enemy.

I felt sorry for him. He was a man in his late-twenties, a career soldier who had lost his glory. I couldn't help thinking that he probably had family, parents, siblings, a wife, or girlfriend. I sensed his sadness and fear over whether he would ever see them again.

Shabtai offered him water. He must have been dehydrated, as he gulped the contents of the whole canteen down in a few long mouthfuls.

We drove back to the temporary base on the sideroad to leave our POW with the support unit.

Shabtai told him to get down, and he slowly climbed down the tank to the ground. A few soldiers came closer and started yelling at him in Arabic. He dropped to his knees and lay face down on the sand. The soldiers kicked him brutally a few times and tied his hands behind his back.

It was an ugly scene, and didn't make sense to me. We, the fighters at the frontline, the ones who had sacrificed the most, could respect our enemies and see them as human beings. At the same time, the military administration and service soldiers treated him with much hate and viciousness.

On our way back to the defense line, Shabtai told me about his conversation with the Egyptian officer. He was one of the artillery observer officers responsible for directing the artillery fire toward our battalion in the most accurate and precise manner. His unit had deserted him when his commander received an urgent order to change assignments.

Our battalion left the line, towing the four damaged tanks to the night camp at sunset. We arrived at the site and started the nightly routine of equipping and preparing our tanks for the next day's battle efficiently and in a timely manner.

My jaw was still painful. I couldn't eat or chew on anything. I could only drink water from the canteen and talk slowly. So, at that time, I wasn't taking any shortcuts with the ammo loading.

CHAPTER 8

Repairs and Maintenance, October 12–13, 1973

I opened my eyes. The sun was already high in the sky, warming us up softly after the chill of the night. Most of the soldiers in our company were still in their sleeping bags. I touched my jaw, opened and closed my mouth to check the pain level, and realized it was manageable.

Maybe I will be able to eat something today.

After fasting for more than twenty-four hours, I was famished. I opened a can of sweetcorn and ate every kernel, slowly, enjoying every bite, including the juice. It tasted heavenly and was satisfying.

Yoav was awake, too.

"What's going on, Yoav?" I asked him. "Why are we still asleep? What are the plans for today?"

He gave a quick grin. "We have a day off today. We'll stay here for repairs and maintenance. We must fix the damaged tanks, electronics, and broken mechanical systems. Also, get ammo supplies, food, new machine guns, and technical support for communication issues. Some teams complained about radio problems. Shabtai will be very busy organizing and coordinating these activities."

"What communication problems do we have?" I asked.

"I heard numerous helmets are not functioning or have an intermittent connection, and some radio transceivers have broken down."

I smiled at Yoav. "I'm all in for the day-off. I need this break."

Shabtai called all the company crews for a short meeting. "Guys, we have twenty-four hours to perform a full, standard weekly maintenance. All tanks must be in tip-top condition and ready to ride long distances.

We might cross the Suez Canal soon. First, I want a list of all malfunctioning items, including communication systems, ASAP. We should get a supply to replace missing or damaged equipment." Shabtai paused to let us absorb his words.

"In addition to the weekly maintenance, you should test tank systems, replace all defective units and parts, deep clean and calibrate weapon systems, and check adjustments. Our task is to restore everything to full functionality before our next assignment. You know what to do, so let's start," he finished.

I decided to start with the machine guns. First, I checked each one to ensure it wasn't loaded, disassembled it from its base, and lined them all up on top of the turret, one gun at a time. Then, I placed them carefully above the front wheel on top of the mudguard and stepped down from the tank.

A weapons cleaning spot was designated on the west side of the camp. I carried the co-axial machine gun, a set of brushes, a cleaning rod, and wiping rugs to the makeshift table of shell boxes positioned one on top of the other. I disassembled the first of the guns and placed it in a cleaning solution—a mixture of oil and kerosene—for a few minutes. This was the dirtiest of the three machine guns since it was the most used.

It took me over an hour to brush and clean all their parts, which had been covered in dust and gunpowder soot, the foremost reasons for firearm malfunction. I assembled the pieces, checked their functionality, oiled the guns, and set their final calibration.

It was already noon when I had finally finished with the three machine guns and installed them back on the tank.

Ami had just finished his maintenance tasks, like greasing the tank wheels, checking the track links and their tensions, and cleaning the dust filters.

"Hey, Amir," he said when he saw me. "Did you finish your dirty job? We waited for you to have lunch. Today we've got some special battle rations." He smirked.

"Yeah, I know. Tins of sweetcorn, corned beef, goulash, a package of Halva, sardines, crackers, and for dessert…" I paused for dramatic effect, "sweet pineapple." I laughed.

"No," Ami said. "This time, there is a surprise. This ration is for Friday dinner, and contains a tin with a fully cooked chicken inside. Also, some fruits and vegetables."

"Really?" I asked in surprise. "That's cool. After a week of eating the same food, whatever this tastes like, it sounds good," I said, grinning.

We started a small fire using wood from the ammunition boxes, punctured the top of the tins containing the whole chickens and the goulash, and placed them at the center of the woodfire. After a while, steam started to rise from the small holes we'd made in the tins, and we knew they were hot. We took them off the heat and opened the lids. It was delicious, one of the best meals we'd had in a long while.

After that satisfying lunch, we continued preparing the tank for our next mission until it turned dark. I cleaned the inside of the turret of sand, dust, and empty cartridges. Then, I oiled the cannon breech, tested the electrical firing circuit, and verified that the ammunition storage cells at the turret and the hull floor were fully loaded.

By then, it was already time to go to sleep. I got into my sleeping bag but wasn't able to fall asleep. I tossed and turned, thinking about home.

What's going on there? How are my mother and brother doing? Was my father called for duty? Do they know where I am? I hoped they hadn't tried to find any information from my previous unit. They were gone.

I wished I could call and tell them that I was fine, I was alive. But there were no phones or any other ways of communicating with them.

I woke up in the morning, and Ami looked at me and said, "No need to rush. The technicians need to complete more maintenance chores, so we'll only get going at noon. Rumor has it that we'll use the floating rolling bridge to cross the canal."

"Great!" I said cheerfully. "Now I can take my time. You know how long it takes me to get ready. Luckily, I finished all my duties yesterday."

But there was one more task remaining. We needed to calibrate the physical cannon position with the gunner periscope aiming system. To my surprise, each company had only one boresight tool. We passed it over from one tank to another after completing the calibration.

It took us a long time to finish, and no moving order arrived.

We stayed for another night at the camp.

CHAPTER 9

Holding Line of Defense, October 14, 1973

"All crews immediately go to your tanks and be ready to move in ten minutes," I heard a loud voice say, breaking the morning's peace.

We stopped all activities, placed the tools inside the external storage bins, and jumped into the tank, ready to move. Some drivers had already started their engines, waiting for the command to move.

Shortly after the announcement, Shabtai arrived and gave Ami the order to follow 3B in the same battle formation as before.

Ami started the tank and moved forward.

"What's going on, Shabbi?" I heard Yoav asking. "What's the rush, all of a sudden?"

In his typically calm way, Shabtai answered. "Our frontline, held by the Tiran tanks force, is collapsing, and they have asked for immediate help. They've already lost a few tanks to Egyptian armored forces and have almost reached their breaking point."

"What's Tiran force?" I asked Shabtai.

"These are modified T-54 and T-55 tanks, which the Arab armies abandoned during the Six Days War. We added new 105 mm main guns, new engines, and other minor changes, and named them Tiran. The unit was incorporated into the Armored Corps."

"And how should we tell them apart from the Egyptian tanks?" I asked.

"The main gun fume extractor on the Egyptian tanks is at the end of the cannon, while on our cannons, it's in the middle, as we all know," Shabtai answered.

I then recalled that in one of the classes at the Academy, the instructor showed us pictures of the soviet tanks T-54 and T-55 and a photo of our modified Tiran to teach us the difference.

Our battalion was now on the move in the direction of the west. Over thirty tanks created a cloud of dust that rolled above the ground like a long, thick snake.

By now, I felt better. My head didn't hurt anymore, and though my jaw was still swollen, I could eat and drink. I was now one of the team. Ami and Yoav had started appreciating my skills, sense of responsibility, honesty, and the fact that I would always complete my duties and tasks on time. As the tank commander, Shabtai cared about the bonding of his crewmen; he asked me to join the team whenever he saw me alone. It was important for me, as for him, that I became an integrated part of the crew, not an outsider. As a tank team, we depended on each other and needed to perform as one to survive the war.

"Braz Stations, this is Braz Sunray. In ten minutes, we'll meet the Tiran force. They've established a line of defense on a few hills west of us. Our orders are to reinforce and hold the line without letting the Egyptian forces break through. We will work together side by side with the Tiran force. Out," the commander radioed.

Reinforcing should be an easy task. Adding our thirty-something tanks to their force will make us a mighty, deadly power.

Standing on my chair, I felt the hot breeze against my face, drying my sweat. We passed a narrow trail and then turned sharply into rough terrain made up of bumpy dunes. The tank rocked like a boat in a stormy sea. Shabtai and I held tight with both hands, trying not to smash our ribs against the steel turret hatches.

"Slow down," Shabtai shouted to Ami.

We turned back to the trail and again moved fast. We had to arrive as soon as possible.

I heard the loud explosions and saw the dark clouds of smoke ahead of us. It was a massive attack, and the sickening stench of war filled the air. A moment later, our line of defense appeared on the horizon, covered with smoke. Heavy artillery dropped on the hilltop, and a few Tiran tanks were on fire.

Suddenly, I saw a few Tiran tanks backing up, turning 180 degrees, and fleeing their spots on the hill. They moved fast toward us.

"What are they doing? Where are they going? Why don't they wait for us?" I asked Shabtai. This was an unbelievable sight.

He didn't answer. But the tightness of his jaw had told me everything.

I waved to the commander of the first Tiran, which approached us fast, and then passed us, moving away from us. He didn't signal back. Instead, he turned his head down and averted his eyes so as not to meet ours. The tank continued driving past us. A couple of other Tirans followed.

Shabtai raised a flag, signaling them to stop, follow us back to the line of defense, and fight back the Egyptians' attack. They ignored him and drove away.

They look beaten. Defeated. They're running for their lives. It doesn't make any sense. We came here to help them, and they desert the line? This is not the kind of behavior expected from IDF soldiers!

All the values I was raised on were collapsing like a house of cards. The facial expressions and gestures of our soldiers reminded me of those of the Egyptian officer, the POW we had captured the other day. Despair, fear, hopelessness, and humiliation were written all over their countenances. Only these were our soldiers.

★★★

"Braz stations, this is Braz Sunray. Go full speed up the hill, 1,500 meters ahead, and reinforce the deserted defense line. Fire immediately at the enemy. We must take the hilltop before the enemy does. Fire at will. I repeat, fire at will."

Oh, God! Whoever captures those chains of low hills first will control the whole area below. The other side will be fully exposed and annihilated.

The tension was unbearable. No one uttered a word inside the tank or over the radio. Our survival depended on who would seize and hold the low mountains first. It would be over in a matter of minutes.

Shabtai promptly gave his orders. "Ami, full speed to the hills. Go slightly right to leave enough space for Platoon Three. Yoav, be ready! Target the tanks first. Use APDS. Amir, load the cannon with APDS now."

I loaded the cannon with an APDS shell and announced, "Cannon is loaded." Then I went to the machine gun and loaded a round into the chamber. "Machine gun is loaded."

I stood back on my chair and looked around. We were about 800 meters from the hills, and I could already see the dense smoke of our burning Tiran tanks. They shook violently with the explosions of their ammo and were starting to break apart. Some turrets were scattered on the sand.

It was a scene from Hell. All around were the giant, lifeless corpses of tanks.

Our tank reached the hill in a couple of minutes. Shabtai slowed Ami down and told him to climb to a turret-down position carefully.

I was shocked by what I saw. Dozens of Egyptian tanks were at a range of 400–500 meters from us, trying to reach the hilltop ahead of us. We couldn't use our advanced, precise long-range firing system.

It felt like watching an old western movie, in which the first to pull the trigger would live, but this was for real. It was about our life or death.

★★★

I jumped inside the turret, ready to load shells, and listened for Shabtai's commands.

"Ami, go a few meters ahead to hull-down. Stop. Yoav, can you see the tank 500 meters ahead? Fire. Fire."

Shabtai turned the turret, and in two seconds, Yoav announced, "Fire," to warn the crew, and the cannon released its first shell. There wasn't much aiming involved in such close proximity. The enemy tank covered most of the telescope sight.

I immediately loaded the second one and called, "Loaded."

"How could I have missed?" I heard Yoav say. "They drive too fast."

"Look! They're retreating," Shabtai responded. "Their commander probably realized we got to the hills first. Hey, they're turning to our left," he said and turned the turret, aiming at one of the tanks.

"On target," Yoav said. Shabtai gave the fire command, and Yoav released the second shell.

I heard the deafening blast of a close explosion.

"It's a target," Yoav called.

Shabtai confirmed and told Ami to drive back to a turret-down position.

★★★

I stepped on my chair and watched. Thirty Egyptian tanks were already on fire after being hit by our battalion tanks. The rest were retreating fast and soon disappeared around the hill.

Shabtai and I were scanning around for new threats when suddenly, I noticed a civilian car moving toward us from the center of the killing zone. It was so surreal! *What is a sedan doing here? Driving to nowhere, in the Sinai desert, between two battling armies?*

At that point, the car didn't pose any real danger. We had enough time to aim at it and shoot. But the car continued driving and came closer and closer.

Shabtai radioed the company commander, asking what to do.

He got a short reply, "Destroy it."

I wasn't comfortable with the command. "Maybe they are civilians or our soldiers trying to escape the Egyptian forces?"

Shabtai gave me a long look and asked again for confirmation.

The answer was, "There are no civilians or IDF soldiers here. Destroy the target."

I loaded the cannon with a HESH round, usually chosen for soft targets, and Yoav fired. The shell passed above the car, and I loaded the second round.

"Stop fire," Shabtai ordered. "Target destroyed."

I got on my chair and looked down through my binoculars. The vehicle had turned into a ball of fire. Pieces of twisted, burned, smoking metal spread all around. I didn't see any movement.

It was a terrible sight, but in a way, I felt relieved; it wasn't us who had destroyed the car.

All of a sudden, an inexplicable image ran through my mind; I imagined that a few reserve troops had been posted at the Bar-Lev line when the war broke out. They had managed to hide from the attacking Egyptian army, and when it was safe to escape, they got into their car and drove east toward our forces. I could even feel their joy to see us, IDF forces, their saviors. Instead, they met their death.

The battle was over.

I sat on the turret above my cell and stared at the killing zone. Observing the destruction, feeling the pain and the agony which was radiating from the valley below, I went numb. *Are my emotions, my reactions to these horrific scenes, gradually fading away?* I wondered. *Does this mean that I am slowly turning into a tough soldier? Do I care less? Is this right?*

I had no answer.

CHAPTER 10

Rest and Recovery,
October 15, 1973

Early morning. The sun's warmth penetrated my sleeping bag and slowly wiped away the night's coldness. I had a little more time to nap before the temperature rose, which would make it too hot to stay inside the sleeping bag. I slowly crawled out, stretched my body, and put my boots on. My team had already eaten their breakfast of sweetcorn, sardines, and crackers, the most popular morning dish.

Shabtai was the early bird out of all of us and had just returned from the officers' briefing. He sat with us on the sand at the west side of the tank, where it was shaded, and the four of us had a lazy, comfortable, friendly conversation. I was part of the group, not just the replacement for the loader they missed, but my own person, an individual. And I liked it. It gave me a sense of comradeship, of being one of the team, something I'd missed since leaving the friends I'd made at the Academy.

We talked about our families back home, with whom none of us had had any contact since the beginning of the war. They must have been very concerned about our well-being. We exchanged some personal information, and my sense of loneliness disappeared. I could even laugh at the banter between Yoav and Ami.

"Shabtai," Yoav said, "What news from the VIP meeting?"

Shabtai smiled. "I knew you would be the one to ask. So, we've got our missions for today and tomorrow. Today is a rest day for reorganization and maintenance. The main Adjutancy officer will arrive soon with letters from home, and it'll be an opportunity for you to send word back to let your families know you're okay. Also, we should wash. I know we don't have standing showers, but at least shampoo your hair and wash your face. We have enough water for that, and…" he paused and chuckled, "I have a mirror if any of you want to stare at your ugly faces."

"In the afternoon, the division commander will give a pep-talk to our unit. After that, we have a show from our national singer." He mentioned a name and waited for our reactions, but we just smiled without much enthusiasm.

"Before noon," Shabtai continued, "We have to prepare the tanks for a long ride. So, grease all the wheels, check oil and tracks, and do what you need to. The last thing we want is to break down in the middle of nowhere."

"Ok, so that's today, but what's the plan for tomorrow? Any rumors, Shabtai?" Ami asked.

"Some officers believe that we'll cross the Suez Canal tomorrow morning to go behind the Third Division of the Egyptian army and cut their supply lines," Shabtai answered.

No one said a word or asked any other questions. We became somber.

After finishing my maintenance duties at noon, I decided to wash my face. I took a large bar of dish soap and a 20-liter jerrycan of water and placed them on the tank's mudguard. Then I checked my face in the mirror Shabtai had left for us.

I didn't recognize myself. *Was that guy, covered with a black mask of dirt, me?* Only my hazel eyes looked familiar. I scratched my fingernails lengthways along my cheeks. A layer of dark, greasy carbon stuck underneath my nails without affecting the thick coating over my skin.

It was a really thick layer. Well, we hadn't had a chance to shower. I hadn't washed for a long time—almost 10 days!

I wet the soap bar with water, worked up an extensive lather, and scrubbed my face vigorously with both hands. The water dripped down my face, and the sand underneath me turned black. *Good, it's working.* But when I checked again in the small mirror, nothing had changed. The dirt was solid on my cheeks.

I changed my tactics, taking the bar and scrubbing my face with it directly. The soap became covered with a black film, but it slowly removed

Hair day at a makeshift base.

the grime from my skin. With more water and rubbing, my face returned to its natural color. Then it was time to work on my hair. I rubbed my scalp thoroughly, washed it, and felt clean and refreshed.

I gave my friends the soap and mirror, and they started cleaning too. More and more soldiers washed and cleaned, and suddenly they all looked different, as if new people had arrived at the base, fresh looking with reddish-pink faces.

Shabtai arrived with letters from home, going from one tank to another to deliver them. I saw the happy faces of the soldiers who had got word from home, from wives and kids, fathers or mothers. Some got only one letter, but most received large envelopes containing multiple. Each soldier took his own bundle and walked aside to read in privacy.

Finally, Shabtai reached our tank and gave a pack of letters to Ami and Yoav, but not to me. He looked at me and said, "Sorry, Amir. Nothing for you. You should check with Adjutancy to verify if your name was updated and registered in our unit. Maybe your mail arrived at your old unit."

I was sad and worried. If the military had misplaced me, I might have been considered missing in action by now. And my family would have been devasted by this false information. I could imagine my parents and younger brother sitting in the living room, crying. Neighbors and friends would have come over to offer comfort and say that some MIA soldiers were eventually found safe and sound.

Suddenly, I heard a reporter's voice; he was walking around and interviewing some of the officers and soldiers. "Anyone who wants to send a letter or give me your home phone number, come see me. I will be in Tel-Aviv tonight and can make the calls as soon as I get there to let your family know that I've seen you alive and well," he said.

A few soldiers gathered around him to give him short notes and phone numbers. I joined the line. It was an ideal solution to my situation. *Tonight, my family will know that I am ok.*

He wrote the phone number I gave him in his notebook, and I thanked him.

The man raised his head and said, "You don't need to thank me, this is the least I can do for you. I wish I could do more to express my gratitude to you and your fellow fighters." And he offered me a handshake.

I was surprised. It was the first time I had experienced this attitude. *Gratitude? For what? It is my duty, isn't it?* This was something I had never thought about before.

A truck stopped and unloaded hundreds of parcels of various sizes, shapes, and colors. Some packages were wrapped like gifts with colored paper and ribbons. Colorful drawings decorated others. While most were addressed to "My Hero Soldier" or "My Brave Soldier," some had printed messages saying things like "A Small Gift to our Soldiers."

Soldiers came closer and started picking up packages from the pile, opening them on the spot to discover a plethora of goodies. It was such a nice gesture from the people back home, an incredible treasure, having eaten only tinned food for the past 10 days. The packages contained a mind-blowing amount of chocolate bars, roasted sunflower seeds in bags, packages of bamba, a favorite Israeli peanut snack, biscuits, wafers, dried fruits, all in larger quantities than I could have imagined.

This was customarily done by school kids and families to show the support and gratitude of the home front to the troops at the frontline.

I had done it myself when I was in middle school, during the Six-Day War in 1967.

I looked at the packages, chose one, and returned to my tank to check its contents. I told Ami, Yoav, and Shabtai about the treasure trove.

The package was square like a shoebox, wrapped with colorful paper and decorated on the outside with lovely hand-drawn flowers. I unwrapped the box and opened it. Inside, I found a half-melted chocolate bar, a few chocolate-covered biscuits, a peanut snack, a bag of potato chips, and a letter. Some packages came with notes from the children. Out of curiosity, I opened the folded page of the note first. It was a short, friendly letter.

> Dear soldier,
>
> I'm writing this letter to express my appreciation for you and your friends that protect us and our country from evil enemies wishing to destroy us.
> Words cannot describe how we feel and how thankful we are to you.
> My mother and my younger sister helped me prepare the package. We pray every day for all our soldiers and our nation's safety.
> God be with you and provide a great victory to our nation.
> With God's help, you will return safely.
> Esther
> Sokolov St. 206/6
> Bnei-Brak,
> P.S.—I'm 17 years old and would be glad if you could write me back.

The letter had surprised me...

She is an Orthodox girl from Bnei-Brak and has written such a letter. I'd never had any interaction with that community. My education was far from religious. It was about Zionism and Socialism, but not about religion. These Orthodox Jews had always been part of our history but didn't seem to belong to the new, modern State of Israel. I'd always thought of them as not caring much about the future of our Zionist state. And yet, this young Orthodox girl had sent me a friendly letter and was worried about the country and us, the soldiers.

I must write her back. For sure, I thought.

Ami and Yoav looked over my shoulder at the letter and started teasing me like two older brothers.

"Is it the letter from the candy box?"

"Who wrote it?"

"Ha, she's seventeen years old. Good find, Amir!"

"What?...She is an Orthodox girl? Don't write back. You're wasting your time."

I didn't respond. Instead, I went to the Adjutancy area, took a few postcards and a pen, and returned to the tank.

First, I wrote to my parents to let them know I was fine. Then I wrote a separate letter to my younger brother, whom I loved more than anything, though I had never said that to him. He was the free spirit of our family, and at the young age of eleven, he never followed rules and antagonized my mother all the time. He was animated and full of jest, always surrounded by friends. The opposite of me, and I admired him for that.

Then it was time for the more complicated of my tasks. *What could I write to that girl, Esther, with whom I have nothing in common?* Then it came to me.

> Dear Esther,
> Thank you for your lovely package. I appreciate everything that you put in it and enjoyed it tremendously.
> I'm a tank commander cadet serving now as a loader. We're somewhere in the Sinai desert, not far from the Suez Canal. Today, after a few days of battling the Egyptian forces to hold our defense lines, we got a rest day.
> I was happy to read about how much you care about us, and I would like to continue our correspondence.
> Amir
> Service Number 2166555
> P.O. box 1953
> Division 162, IDF

I put the rest of the blank postcards inside the loader cell, deciding to write my family daily and mail them henever possible. I dropped my letters to my family and Esther in the "Send" mailbox near the Adjutancy area.

In the afternoon, just before the meeting with the division commander, I saw Shabtai standing beside a jeep and talking with a high-ranking officer.

He noticed me and called, "Hey Amir, come meet my father, David. He came to visit me." Shabtai seemed happy.

"Hi, I'm Shabtai's loader," I introduced myself to the man.

Shabtai briefly told him about some of the days we'd spent in battle, the captured Egyptian officer, and the handgun he took from the POW. He sounded excited.

After his father left, Shabtai told me that his father was a war hero. During the War of Independence in 1948, he was the one who had stopped the Syrian tank at the gates of Kibbutz Degania. Still, the army never credited him for his bravery, as a few other soldiers had claimed credit for the same act of courage.

★★★

I left Shabtai and went to find a better seat closer to the top of the dune, where the singer's performance was about to begin. A small, square wooden stage, erected earlier, was being flooded with bright light from two light towers. Two large speakers connected to a powerful amplifier had been placed on either side of the stage.

One of the officers stood in front of the microphone and introduced the singer. "Hi, guys. I'm happy to present to you our most famous war singer, who will be performing a vast collection of songs which we all know and love. Please welcome our great National War Singer," he shouted enthusiastically into the mike.

Loud whistles and handclapping followed his words.

The singer took the microphone in her hands. With a frown on her face, she spurted out "I'm not a "war singer," I'm a "peace singer," or you can call me the "soldiers' singer." I hate when you call me a "War Singer." I don't believe in wars. All I want is peace. Peace and love."

An unpleasant silence descended upon the vast sandy area. But the singer either didn't notice or didn't care. She started singing songs of hope, prayers for peace, and other tunes from our parents' era. She finished with the only truly beautiful piece, the symbol of the Six-Day War—"Jerusalem of Gold."

I wasn't too excited about her performance, especially after her opening statement. I had expected to hear songs that would cheer me up, not lyrics about her hope for an unattainable peace or about fallen soldiers in past wars. Besides, I loved modern Israeli pop music and the young singers of the 70s, and couldn't relate to the old tunes she had chosen.

I was also disappointed with her outburst. We were in a war which had been forced on us, which threatened our existence as a nation and a state, and I didn't appreciate her pacifist protests.

What nonsense! She's totally out of touch with the harsh reality we're facing these days. Doesn't she understand that her job as an entertainer is to boost our optimism and cheer us up? We're in this war not out of our own choice but out of necessity, to protect our families and our country. As the Army of the People, it's our duty and obligation. If we could choose peace over this terrible war, we wouldn't hesitate. There'd be no need for a character like her to convince us. After the war, it will be the time to sing about peace, love, and the good life.

★★★

It was already evening when the division commander, Major General Avraham Eden, aka Bren, came to talk to us and explain the missions for our division.

The audience was quiet when he arrived, followed by a few high-ranking officers. We all stood at attention and saluted him. The commander was greatly respected. He saluted back to show his appreciation and laid out the plans for crossing the Suez Canal the following day.

"Our strategy includes three elements:

Tomorrow morning all tanks will ride toward the Suez Canal.

A floating roller bridge will be waiting for us at the crossing point.

The infantry will hold and protect the crossing point."

He ended his short briefing as we listened in silence. Nobody raised any questions. The commander saluted us again, climbed his jeep with the two officers, and drove off.

I stood up from the sand spot I'd been sitting on and slowly went back to our tank. I removed my boots to let my feet breathe, took off my uniform, and entered inside my sleeping bag on top of the transmission plate.

Like everyone else around me, I was worried about our next mission.

Aug. 1973 – The author sitting on top of the turret of a *Shot-Kal* tank after completing his Basic Tank Training.

The author commanding a *Shot-Kal* tank after the Yom Kippur War.

The author is in front of his tank at a makeshift battalion base.

The author's platoon after the Yom Kippur War.

Military practice out in the sand.

Sunrise in the desert.

Even in the desert, there are rainstorms.

The author's platoon commander after the war and lifelong friend, Itzhak.

Finally, during a break between practices, the platoon commanders get together (after the Yom Kippur War).

The author commanding his tank, west of the Suez Canal.

The author and his tank team fueling their tank after the war.

CHAPTER 11

New Day, October 16, 1973

Morning. The sun was already high in the sky when I woke up, sweaty. Being tucked inside the sleeping bag was unbearable. I crawled out, folded the sleeping bag, stuffed it inside the external storage bins on the turret, and went to wash my face.

I saw Shabtai organizing his essential morning kit. "Why aren't we moving?" I asked.

"There is a delay in crossing the canal since the roller bridge is not ready for us yet," he answered.

The Floating Roller Bridge was supposed to be the IDF's brilliant, most secret invention. But in fact, it was well-known to all. It had been

Crossing the Suez Canal using the rollers floating bridge. (Wikimedia)

designed, engineered, and built a couple of years after the Six-Day war in preparation for crossing over the Suez Canal and into Egypt in a future war.

"What do you mean?" I asked.

"It broke apart when the tanks attempted to pull it over the dunes and to the crossing point. It seems nobody paid much attention to the topography of the Sinai desert," Shabtai said and shrugged.

Great, we're getting another day of rest.

I wasn't excited about crossing the canal or another day of combat, but of course, I didn't express those feelings to my team members. It would be a shameful display of weakness. Brave soldiers were expected to fight and face the battlefield without hesitation or fear.

CHAPTER 12

Ambushed, October 17, 1973

"We are leaving in fifteen minutes," I heard the announcement.

Shabtai approached our tank and said, "Let's organize our stuff and get ready to move. We have a long ride to the Bitter Lake area. That area leads to the crossing point and must be reinforced."

We climbed to the tank, each going to his place. Ami started the engine. I stood on the loader chair, put on my helmet, and checked the radio communications with the team. Shabtai directed Ami to join the moving tanks of our Braz company, at the end of the line.

I covered my eyes with the dust goggles, removed my Seiko watch from my wrist, and placed it inside the turret. I didn't want to damage this gift from my parents.

The horrible sights that we saw on our way to the Bitter Lake served as heart-wrenching evidence of the war. We passed one of our destroyed artillery units. Four blackened skeletons of 155mm cannons, now just chunks of twisted, melted metal, were surrounded by tar-black, burned sand. One of the cannons pointed to the sky. From the middle of the cannon to its end, the metal barrel had split into five stripes that looked like the giant petals of a gruesome flower, as if it were crying toward the sky for mercy, and forgiveness for its fatal failure. The shell had probably exploded inside the barrel and destroyed all the parts and ammunition without sparing any of the crew.

Burned tanks and armored vehicles were scattered around, damaged beyond repair. Each one carried its own tragic story of loss of humans and machines. The loss of memories from the past and the end of hopes and dreams for the future, leaving behind devastated loved ones.

★★★

We reached the Great Bitter Lake area, with its flat, white, powdery surface and lack of proper battle positions for tanks. And this was to be our post, where we would need to keep free from the enemy.

I put on my binoculars, watching for any sign of the enemy. Nothing. I couldn't see any imminent threat.

Suddenly, something passed a few centimeters above our heads; it felt like a fishing line had been flung over us.

What is that? My brain collected the information at hand and tried to process it quickly. It was a guided missile aimed at our tank and had missed us by a few inches. "Sagger just missed us," I said into the radio. "I saw the line above our head."

Shabtai didn't hesitate. "Back and to the right," he commanded Ami.

I was surprised at how quickly Ami reacted, moving the tank back to escape another incoming missile. Egyptian Saggers were targeting us, and we had no place to hide.

One of the tanks from our company took a direct hit and started to burn. Two of its crew jumped out and rolled themselves around on the sand to extinguish the fire.

Shabtai threw a smoke grenade, but it didn't do much to disguise our TANK.

"Fire ahead of you with your machine guns," the radio screamed.

I tried to fire, but my machine gun was obstructed. The sand and the heavy dust jammed the movement of the rounds. Shabtai's Browning 0.3" didn't work either, and the co-axial was stuck too.

Immediately, I jumped inside the turret to repair the co-axial. At that moment, it was the most important tool. I removed the co-axial from its base, disassembled, cleaned, and oiled it part by part. In under two minutes, I had it fully reassembled. I put it back into the bracket, loaded the rounds of ammo, pulled the charging handle, and called, "Machine gun is loaded."

Shabtai aimed the cannon in the direction of the enemy and ordered, "1,200 ahead, a tree beside a long dune."

Yoav spotted the point, set the range, zeroed in, and said, "On."

"Fire," Shabtai ordered.

The machine gun, now well-tuned, started to shoot fluidly, and targeted an area at a range of approximately 1,200 meters.

Shabtai called over to me, "My machine gun doesn't work either." He removed it from its mounting and transferred it to me. Again, I took it apart, cleaned it, oiled it, set all the parts back together, and handed it to Shabtai. By now, two of our machine guns were shooting.

More and more of the tanks in our battalion had begun firing, and the skyline was lit up by hundreds of bright red lines of tracer bullets.

Shabtai looked at me and said, "Great job. You're an excellent loader."

"Braz, this is Sunray. Take your armored infantry and outflank the enemy on both sides."

I noticed the armoured infantry moving ahead at full speed. The chance of being hit by a missile is lower when you are on the move.

The battle was over a few minutes later, and we stayed at the site until sunset, then moved to our night parking destination.

The leading tank was that of the battalion commander, followed by his three companies. The convoy, with its tanks roaring noisily, created a long snake of dust.

I was in position, helping navigate the tank in dark conditions and watching for any danger ahead. I was relaxed. The full moon helped us to see the tanks in front of us and the military blackout markers, red lights, or, as they were called, "cat eyes," assisted us too.

We stayed on full alert, keeping a safe distance between the tanks to avoid a nasty accident. A fender bender could cause massive damage and decommission the tanks. But everything went smoothly and relatively quietly.

We entered a narrow wadi between two long, steep hills. The tanks followed each other along the path, slowly, like a flock of geese marching along a meadow; it seemed like it was going to be a peaceful drive to our destination. Some tanks had already passed through the valley.

Ami drove the tank carefully and made me feel safe.

Suddenly the radio started up. "This is 1. We are under attack. 1B was hit."

I was immediately on full alert. My muscles tightened, and my heart rate went through the roof as I looked around to identify the threat.

"This is 1. 1C drove around 1B and went over a mine."

"We're stuck."

"We can't move ahead," the radio screamed.

"This is Braz Sunray. Fire immediately toward the hills."

The dark sky was lit up by hundreds of tracer bullets, Egyptian rockets, and RPGs, which shot at us from all directions.

I lowered myself into the turret, with only the top of my head exposed, and watched the terrifying situation. We, in our tank, couldn't do anything. We had got stuck in between two tanks when our convoy stopped moving.

"Amir, bring me a smoke grenade and start firing from your MG," Shabtai ordered.

I tried to find the source of the enemy's fire but couldn't identify it. I loaded the machine gun and started shooting toward the hills around the tank, trying to force the enemy into hiding. Over the busy radio communications, I heard a few more tanks had been struck. Some had run over mines and now couldn't move, and others had collided with them as they were trying to escape the trap.

What a screw-up. We're so fucked. It's just a matter of time until the Egyptian commando gets us too.

"This is loader of Braz Sunray. We're struck. Braz Sunray is wounded. I repeat, Braz Sunray is wounded," I heard the radio blare.

Shabtai responded. "All Braz stations, this is Braz Sunray's deputy. I'm taking over Braz Sunray's duties."

Then, through our internal communications, he ordered: "Ami, we must get out of the convoy line. Drive ahead half a meter, being careful not to hit the tank in front of us."

And when our driver followed the instruction, Shabtai said, "Now turn right, in place." The tank turned its two tracks in opposite directions. The left track slowly moved ahead while the right moved in reverse. The tank started to rotate in place like a gigantic, spinning screw.

"Continue until we're facing the hill on our right side," Shabtai further directed Ami.

Ami turned the tank until it was facing the hill.

"It's very steep," Ami said. "I'm not sure we can climb it at this angle."

"Do everything that's possible. We must cross this hill. Staying here is not an option!" Shabtai replied. "This is Braz deputy," Shabtai radioed in to our company. "I'm driving up the hill, marking myself with a few rounds of tracer bullets in the direction of the sky. Follow my tracks. If I am hit or detonate a landmine, continue moving and pass me on my right until you get to the other side of the hill. Over."

I knew that I must stay low. The enemy bullets and rockets whistled around us constantly. We'd be fully exposed when Shabtai used the tracer bullets he'd promised.

The tank started to move up the hill. It was a very steep angle, but Shabtai and Ami maneuvered it successfully, turning right and left according to the rough terrain. I supported myself as best I could with both hands on the loader hatch.

We continued to move upward, and a few tanks followed us. Others turned in different directions, trying to escape the ambush by all means necessary, desperate to avoid being sitting ducks in a kill zone.

The angle of the hillside became increasingly extreme and difficult to navigate as we neared the top. Ami floored the gas pedal, but the tank hardly moved. Its engine screamed, trying to transfer any bit of power to the tracks to push forward. We were almost at the maximum climbing angle capability of the tank. My shoulders were squeezed painfully against the hatch.

Just a few more meters were between us and the top. The tank crawled along, one meter after another until finally, we made it. As we passed the summit, the angle changed immediately, like we were on a giant seesaw. We dropped down a sharp slope.

Flashes of explosions, the loud echoing of machine gun shots, and the blasts of cannon fireballs in the valley had vanished, had been left behind. Our tank was safe and out of the kill zone.

A sense of relief washed over me...*I'm so lucky. What a scare! We were so close to being slaughtered!*

Ami drove the tank slowly downhill until we reached a vast plateau. Three of the tanks from our company followed us.

"This is Gir Sunray. Wherever you are, gather all your forces and continue to our night camp location," I heard the battalion commander instructing over the radio.

Shabtai looked at me and shook his head. "That won't be easy," he said. "Except for these three tanks behind us, the others are scattered all around." Then he radioed his command. "All Braz stations, this is Braz deputy. I will shoot short rounds up to the sky to mark my location. Approach me ASAP."

"This is 2A. The sky's full of tracers. Can't find your direction."

"This is Braz deputy. I'll aim my searchlight at the sky for ten seconds," Shabtai said.

A long, powerful beam of light lit the sky for a few seconds, fully exposing our location.

"This is 2A. I can see you. 2B is with me, and we're on the move. Will be at your location in ten."

Slowly, we gathered our company. We counted eight tanks but didn't know the fate of three others. Shabtai started leading the company to the camping area at 2:00 a.m.

CHAPTER 13

The Crossing, October 18, 1973

I felt somebody shaking my shoulder but ignored it. I was too exhausted to respond.

It's not morning yet. I want to sleep a little more. Just ignore it and move on to a different dream.

Again. Another shake, but now I also heard a voice. "Amir, wake up, wake up...we must prepare for departure in fifteen minutes."

Fuck it! It's not a dream. I opened my eyes and checked my watch. 5:45 a.m.! I turned my head and looked out from my sleeping bag. It was still dark, but I could hear the rumble of tanks starting their engines and see them turning their headlights on.

I crawled out of my sleeping bag slowly and put on my boots. Then I took the jerrycan of water to wash my face and noticed Yoav and Ami were busy preparing to leave.

Shabtai wasn't around. Since he had also taken on the company commander's duties on top of his deputy's tasks, he had more responsibilities and less time.

At 6:00 a.m., I was standing on my loader chair, ready to move. Company A started to move out slowly, following the battalion commander's tank. Tank after tank joined the convoy and adopted a standard battle pattern after a few hundred meters. Dark smoke from the diesel, combined with the heavy dust, wrapped around me and obscured my view. I cleaned my dust goggles and stood straight on my chair beside Shabtai.

Shabtai looked at me. "Ready?" he asked, his eyes red and hardly open, his lips tightened, and his face looking suddenly thinner than before.

"Yes, I am. I managed to sleep for about three hours, and now I'm fine," I said.

"Lucky you," Shabtai muttered.

Company A left the area.

"Are we ready to go?" Shabtai asked the crew.

"Driver is ready," Ami said.

"Gunner is ready," Yoav answered.

"Loader is ready," I said.

We answered one by one, slowly, our voices flat and emotionless.

"Braz stations, this is Braz Sunray. We will move in five. I will lead. Follow me in the standard battle structure. Platoon One on my left, Platoon Two on my right, and Platoon Three at the back."

"Ami, start the engine," Shabtai ordered over the internal communications system.

The tank roared as it woke up, spewing out black clouds of exhaust fumes from its rear.

"Move forward, slowly."

Our tank followed Company A. I stood on my chair, quiet, with arms folded over the hatch to support my body and stop myself from getting injured from jolts caused by the bumpy terrain. My ribs were bruised enough from the previous day when we'd had to climb the steep hill. I was half-asleep. My eyelids felt so heavy that I couldn't keep them open, and I dozed off and then shook myself awake again, still standing on the loader chair.

The temperatures had risen, melting away the painful, bone-chilling sensation of the cold metal against my skin. It felt so good. The sunrays gently caressed my head and face like a lover's hands, brushing her warm fingers against my shoulders, waking me up with a soft kiss of warmth.

I opened my eyes and stared at the road ahead, my vision still unfocused. The sun had painted the sky with red and orange hues, and the desert slowly revealed itself. The hills around us, which had seemed small and far-off, were now much closer and more visible.

Suddenly I saw a movement, and my whole body was on full alert. But it was nothing. Just yellow-brown, woody stems which had been broken off from the thorny acacia bushes that grew there sporadically.

The dry, dead stalks floated aimlessly in the wild, blowing wind. Nothing seemed to be alive in that forsaken desert.

★★★

The company tanks followed our tank along the hot, black asphalt road. Nothing seemed unusual.

"This is Gir Sunray. We're under air attack. Spread out and stop moving. Use all available rounds and fire at will," the battalion commander radioed.

Shabtai immediately repeated the message to our company. The tanks moved quickly to the left and the right to break up our pattern, and then stopped.

I loaded my machine gun with the 250 rounds from the ammo box and looked to the sky to identify the jets. I immediately heard and then saw four MiGs flying low. The noise was deafening. They were very close. I started shooting, hoping it would have some impact, but I couldn't see what the result was. Thunderous explosions shook the ground around us.

God! We're lucky! They missed us. It's stupid to stand still and shoot at them with these useless 7.62mm machine guns. Fuck! It's scary. It's like we're sacrifices being picked on by these deadly, metal birds of prey, and our survival depends on luck.

I watched the four MiGs climbing up into the sky and returning one by one to create a gigantic, deadly Ferris-wheel formation. This meant that at all times one of the MiGs was in an attack position, while the other was retreating after its last attack. The next plane would then be at its maximum height, and the last would be diving down sharply toward the target.

Massive fireballs exploded loudly, pounding the ground violently again and again. Mushrooms of black smoke, sand, and dust rose from the terrain and were carried in our direction by the wind.

"They're targeting the back of the battalion, where the support teams and supplies are," I heard Shabtai saying.

We used up the first two ammo boxes in a couple of minutes. I dived inside the loader cell and took four additional boxes for Shabtai and I. I dropped them on top of the turret, loaded my machine gun, and continued to shoot, aiming at the imaginary point in the sky that

I believed the MiGs would pass. Nothing. I had to slow down as the machine gun had become scorching hot; the barrel was already bright red and might get damaged if I continued shooting at that rate.

I changed my tactics and paused my shooting every five seconds, but I was still unsuccessful. All of the tanks in the battalion aimed and fired toward the sky without visible results, nothing at all.

It's so frustrating. We're powerless.

Then suddenly, the air raid was over. The MiGs disappeared to the west, leaving us with our ears ringing, covered with a thick layer of dust and sand, and with the blasting noises of more explosions behind us. Our ammunition trucks were on fire. *Oh, God! I'm so lucky! It's unbelievable. How can it be? Am I somehow protected? Why? It's not as if I'm anyone special or have any particularly unique talents.*

"Braz, this is Sunray. Provide a damage report." My headphones, inside the helmet, came alive and brought me back to reality.

"This is Platoon One. No injury and no damage."

"This is Platoon Two. No injury and no damage."

"This is Platoon Three. No injury and no damage."

Shabtai changed to the battalion radio channel and reported, "Gir Sunray, this is Braz Sunray, no casualties or damages."

"To all Gir stations, move at the same pattern immediately. We have no time to waste. All broken and damaged units will be fixed at our next location," the battalion commander ordered.

"What's the rush?" Yoav asked over the internal tank communications.

"The paratroopers cleared the passage to the Suez Canal. We're moving to the Chinese Farm, on the east side of the canal, and north of the Bitter Lake, to cross the Suez Canal," Shabtai answered. "This area was cleared two days ago, but the Egyptians brought more antitank weaponry and slowed down our plans for crossing. We paid heavy losses. Then paratroopers entered the battle, and although they suffered serious casualties, they managed to defeat the Egyptian forces," Shabtai shared his knowledge with us.

★★★

Afternoon.

"We have arrived at Tasa," Shabtai announced.

I looked around and saw an intersection of two single-lane roads crossing each other, and a few tents occupied by service units with their equipment and flags surrounding them. A few soldiers stopped their work and saluted our passing tanks with respect and appreciation. It made me feel good, proud.

The battalion units turned west in the direction of the Suez Canal. Company by company passed the intersection and employed a battle formation.

Heavy smoke from artillery shells darkened the horizon, but its source was still far away. We continued forward when I suddenly noticed an infantry unit passing us, walking in the opposite direction, to the east. I looked at their red paratrooper boots and knew they were the fighters who had cleared out the Chinese Farm passage. They treaded slowly, carrying their gear, and looked exhausted. I scanned their dark, dirty faces, trying to find my best friend from high school, Uri.

Uri and I had gone to the same high school, taken the same classes, and participated in the same after-school activities. And when he told me he wanted to volunteer for the paratrooper brigade, I was the one who had practiced with him, jogging 6 kilometers every night. We were like blood brothers.

I didn't see Uri there.

★★★

We got closer and closer to the canal. The artillery shells continued to drop all around us, but I knew that we would be protected in the tank as long as we didn't take a direct hit.

Shabtai stood as low as possible, with only the top of his head down to his eyes peeking out to navigate for the company of tanks which was following us.

We moved slowly, waiting for our turn to cross the canal. It was already dark, but the sky was illuminated with white parachute flares. The artillery fire never stopped. It sounded like a violent thunderstorm with powerful lightning. Then, we arrived at the crossing point. I looked out, expecting to see the bridge we needed to cross…but there was no bridge. Three large ferries were floating in the water. Each one was made of three small, flat crafts which connected to form a spacious, solid space large enough to carry two tanks. This space had a steel floor and a low railing on both sides.

The last tank from the first company of our battalion started climbing slowly and cautiously onto the ferry, guided by the ferry's operator. The tank moved up to the far edge to leave enough space on the boat for our tank. It was the deputy commander of Company A.

"Ami, can you see the loading ramp?" Shabtai asked.

"Yes" Ami answered. "But I need to open my hatch lid to see the ramp clearly and drive the tank out to the loading deck area."

"Okay," Shabtai said.

Ami climbed onto the ferry loading area, following Shabtai and the ferry operator's instructions. After a few minutes, our tank was on the ferry, and we were ready to cross the Suez Canal.

The shells continued to fall around us. I entered the turret—it was safer inside and I had nothing more to do at that point, not until the ferry reached the other side of the canal. I sat on my chair, and my eyelids dropped. I tried to fight to stay awake, as it wasn't a good time to sleep, but my brain just shut down.

I woke up. It was dark, silent, and I had lost track of time. I stood on my chair and saw that we were still floating on the water but moving in the wrong direction. I looked around. The other two ferries continued to move toward the west bank to unload their tanks.

"What's going on? Why are we going back?" I asked Shabtai.

"We're having mechanical problems. The operators couldn't anchor the ferry at the west bank, so we went back," Shabtai said. "You better go back to sleep. Enjoy it while you can." He smiled at me.

Fuck! It's not good floating on the water with all these shells dropping around us nonstop.

I went down inside my cell and sat on my chair. I was exhausted, and soon after, I fell into a deep slumber.

"Wake up, wake up!" I suddenly heard Shabtai shouting. "We're rolling over. Jump out of the tank. Leave it…now!"

The urgency in his voice woke me up immediately. In seconds, my brain had gone into alert mode, and I pushed myself out of the loader chair and onto the top of the hatch. I sat on the lid and looked around.

The ferry with the two tanks had started to tilt onto its left side. Adrenaline rushed through my body, and my brain processed the dangerous situation like the fastest, highest-performing supercomputer. This life-threatening event would be over in a matter of seconds, and my survival depended on my response.

I can't jump yet.

No. I still have a few more seconds until the tank slides to the edge and flips over.

My best chance of survival is to jump as far as possible from the 50-tonne, plunging mass just before it goes over. Otherwise, I'll be dragged straight down to the bottom of the canal.

I must remove anything heavy and breathe in as much as possible just before I jump. The water will create a vortex which will pull me down when the tank drops into the canal.

I removed my Uzi gun. My helmet was still on my head.

Yoav's chair was below Shabtai's seat, and he could only exit via the commander's hatch.

I heard Yoav shouting at Shabtai.

"Help me out!"

"Hurry up!"

"Let me out…"

Shabtai entered inside the tank quickly and moved toward Yoav.

Yoav's cries sounded desperate.

"Don't block my way."

"HELP ME OUT!"

"LET ME OUT!"

★★★

The tank started to slide slowly to the left edge of the ferry. Its steel tracks squeaked as they scored the ferry's metal deck plate.

The ferry operators jumped into the water from the front and the back of it.

I removed my heavy helmet, which ended my connection to the internal communications system, and was ready to jump.

The tank hit the side rail and slowly tipped over the left side of the ferry.

Don't jump! It's too early. Wait!

When the tank tilts 45 degrees, jump.

Hold tight.

Wait one more second.

I crouched, pushed my heels against the hatch edge, and tightly grabbed the lid behind my back with two hands.

Now! Now the time is right!

I flexed every muscle in my body to the extreme and jumped from the tank turret. I became airborne, hit the water with my back, and sank into the salty, oily seawater of the canal. I pushed myself up, swimming toward the surface as the tank plunged into the water. The massive monster pulled me deep down into the canal; it felt as if heavy weights were tied to my legs.

So dark. So quiet. I can't see or hear anything. How long can I survive without breathing?

I continued pushing up toward the surface, which seemed to be miles away.

Air. Air. I need air!

I felt I couldn't hold my breath anymore; my lungs were screaming for fresh air.

No! I can't give up now.

And bit by bit, I released the air from my lungs into the water, one bubble at a time.

Suddenly, my hands reached into the air, above the surface, and with one last powerful stroke, my head popped out of the water, gasping for air. I opened my mouth like a fish out of water, breathing in and out and filling my lungs with sweet air and oxygen.

Oh, God!…Fresh air.

More.

More.

More.

I gulped the air like a thirsty nomad in the desert and breathed so rapidly that I became lightheaded.

I looked around, not sure where to swim. *Should I go to the east side, or toward the Egyptian's west side to meet our forces that had already crossed the canal?* I decided to go east.

The artillery shelling didn't stop, and a few parachute flares exploded above my head. I flipped over to my back and started to swim. I remembered the stories about the *Eilat* destroyer which had been sunk by Egyptian missiles in October 1967. Most of the sailors were injured internally, gravely injured, by a third missile that had exploded in the sea where the crew jumped off the sinking ship. The shock waves did not harm the soldiers that had swum on their backs.

A few minutes later, I heard loud voices calling in Hebrew, "Any survivors? Anyone here?"

"Yes, I'm here. I'm here," I shouted back.

A *Zodiac* boat with its crew approached me and pulled me up. "Did you see anyone around you?" one of them asked. "Anyone from the tanks, or the ferry operators?"

"No," I answered.

Two soaking-wet survivors from the operator's crew sat silently on the wooden bench. The *Zodiac* turned to the west bank, dropped us off at the dock, and went back to look for more survivors.

"Amir, you are here. Thank God," I suddenly heard Ami's voice.

I looked at him in surprise and couldn't believe he had survived. In an emergency, the driver's location in the tank was the most challenging position to escape.

"Did you see Shabtai or Yoav?" I asked.

"No," he shook his head. "We are the only two survivors from the two tanks," he said.

"It's impossible," I said. "I don't know about Yoav, but Shabtai was the one who alerted us all. He had enough time to jump!" I heard my voice become high and angry.

Ami didn't respond.

I looked down at the black water in front of me, breathing heavily. *No! It didn't happen. They couldn't have drowned. I must find them. They would do the same if I had gone missing.*

I saw the *Zodiac* approaching again. One of the men shook his head at me. No survivors. *Why is everyone giving up on them so easily? So quickly? They must be swimming somewhere in the water. Alive.*

"Shabtai, Yoav, where are you?" I shouted at the water.

Nothing. The ugly, murky water was silent.

"Shabtai, Yoav, where are you?" I shouted again.

A soldier in the *Zodiac* raised his hand. "Hey, you! Stop shouting. You're making too much noise and risking the lives of all of us. Look," his tone softened. "We've searched for survivors many times but couldn't find anyone else. I'm sorry, soldier," he said.

"Can you check again?" I asked.

"I will do now, but you must leave this area," he answered, turning the boat and sailing into the center of the canal.

A tank stopped beside me. I could recognize by its marks that it was that of the company commander of the third battalion.

"Come in and share the loader cell with my loader."

I hesitated. I wasn't yet ready to leave my missing crew members behind.

"I have no time to wait for you, and I can't leave you here. Get inside my tank now," the commander ordered.

I glanced at the water for one last time. It was early morning. All the stars which had been watching over us from the sky had gone, leaving us with the giant red sun that was climbing slowly upwards. I could see the two functioning ferries loading and unloading tanks, but no sign of Shabtai or Yoav.

I climbed in, cold, wet, and dripping seawater, and entered the loader cell. I stood inside while the loader stood on his chair.

"What tank are you from?" the company commander asked me.

"Shabtai's," I answered.

He didn't say a word. Then he gave his driver the command to go ahead and radioed his company to follow him.

CHAPTER 14

New Tank Crew, October 19, 1973

The commander tank stopped for a short break to let the company organize after the canal crossing. My new tank crew climbed down to refresh themselves while I stood on the loader chair.

"Here, take these dry uniforms and change. Take my Uzi gun. I have an AK-47," the commander said with a heavy American accent. He handed me the stuff and left the tank. When he reached the ground, he looked at me and said, "My name is Daniel. What's yours?"

"Amir," I answered.

I was alone inside the tank. I decided to get out and look around. We were parked in a small, wooded area with tall palm trees. After a couple of weeks of seeing only desert scenes, it was like a little piece of paradise.

I took the water jerrycan and put it on the mudguard. Then I peeled off my wet uniform and washed the salty seawater off my body. I've always hated the sensation of saltwater on my skin. I put the clean, dry combat uniform on over my wet body. In the heat of the desert, I knew it would dry quickly.

I was alone and wasn't looking to mingle with the other soldiers. They had gathered in groups and were talking about the tanks which had sunk—the event I'd experienced firsthand. All I wanted at that moment was to be left alone, to try to make sense of what, currently, I couldn't comprehend. I wished I could curl up inside my body like a frightened turtle hiding in its shell and block out any sense of danger, pain, and loss.

Ahh. No good. I must control my emotions, show the toughness I don't possess, and adapt to my new reality.

I went back to the tank and sat motionless and silent on the loader chair, thinking about Shabtai and Yoav, trying to understand why they didn't jump.

Did they drown?

Are they dead?

Everybody seems to believe they both died.

But I could feel their presence in my heart, my mind, just like before the accident…Sadness lodged itself heavily in my chest.

Why did I survive?

BOOM! BOOM! BOOM!

A barrage of artillery shells shook the camping area and then ended as suddenly as it had begun.

I peeked outside the turret and saw crew members running back to their tanks to take shelter.

My new crew jumped in, and we waited for our commander.

He didn't show up.

"Core Sunray, this is Core Deputy. We're waiting for your instructions. Over," the radio suddenly sounded.

"Sunray, this is your deputy. We are waiting for your instructions. Over," the radio announced again.

The loader moved to the commander's chair, took the microphone, and answered, "Core Deputy, this is the loader; Sunray is not here."

The radio went silent.

I stepped on the loader chair and looked outside. A few paramedics ran in our direction, carrying a bloody stretcher with a wounded soldier connected to an IV infusion.

"What's going on?" our loader asked.

"We've had some injuries and one fatality."

"Who's the fatality?"

"Daniel," the paramedic said. "Bits of tiny shrapnel pierced directly into his heart. At first, we couldn't work out how he died. He hardly bled. It was as if there was a small needle in his chest."

"Core stations, this is Core Deputy. I'm taking over Core," the radio said. "We have to leave now. Follow me in a standard battle pattern. We will stop soon to re-assign new crew members."

"I can be the tank commander," said the other loader. "I was a commander during my military service, and we have a new loader here, so we're a complete crew."

No one said a word. Losing one of your team was very tough emotionally.

The tank loader took his gear and personal weapon, moved to the commander's seat, put his helmet on, and connected himself to the radio system.

"Guys, this is Boaz. How do you hear me?" he asked.

"Driver. Sound is clear."

"Gunner. Sound is clear."

I put Daniel's helmet on, fitted it to my head, and answered, "Loader. Sound is good."

Our new tank commander looked at me and extended his arm for a handshake. "We didn't have time before. My name is Boaz."

I shook his hand. "I'm Amir," I said.

"Tom is the driver, and Dov is the gunner," he said.

★★★

We moved south, leaving the hellish paradise behind us, marking the moist dirt with the tank's steel tracks as we went.

I stood on the loader's chair and watched the way for any sign of danger or enemy. We passed through green agricultural fields, palm trees, and small farmers huts, all of which seemed to be alive and flourishing, a celebration of life. The sights reminded me of my home, a small agricultural boarding school in central Israel, which was surrounded by green fields of peppers and cucumbers, red tomato beds, orchards of avocados, mangos, oranges, pecans, and in between them all, plots of feed crops.

These familiar sights washed over my soul, relaxed my spirit, allowed me to let my guard down, and filled me with a sense of security, as if I was back at home.

My father came to my mind. *Where is he now? Was he drafted into this dreadful war?* I knew my mother was probably worried sick but would never show it; she would act like a lioness protecting her family and loved ones. And my younger brother…how was he dealing with the war at his young age?

★★★

"Core Stations. This is Core Sunray. We will stop shortly to organize and assign new crew members. All tank commanders or acting commanders, gather beside my tank. Other crew members are to stay inside your tanks. End." The radio communication cut into my reveries.

The convoy stopped. Boaz left our tank and walked to the front tank.

"Amir," I heard Boaz call out momentarily after he left, "remove the second radio. It will go to one of the officer's tanks."

I confirmed I'd heard him and removed the second radio which had been connected to the battalion net, leaving the one we used for communications with our company radio net.

Boaz took the radio system and went back to the company commander. He returned after a few minutes.

"Guys, we're now tank 2A," he said. "The plan is to move west and destroy the Egyptian's antiaircraft missile base to allow our air force an open sky and better support for us."

We started to move. After a few minutes, the green pastures of the landscape around the Sweet Water Canal gave way to ugly scenes of the yellowish-white, dead, empty desert.

We moved in a widespread battle formation for a few miles when I suddenly saw an extensive Egyptian military base ahead, with large missiles directed at the sky. Each platform was surrounded by an earth embankment for protection. A few buildings with rotating antennas were scattered around. Steel, concertina wire fencing and narrow ditches which had been dug in a zigzag pattern protected the base from attack by all directions.

As we approached the fences, we weren't met with any fire. It was quiet and looked like a deserted base.

Could it be that the Egyptians left their positions when they noticed us coming?

But that was just wishful thinking, and in a brief moment, the whole area shook with the blasting of artillery shells.

Boaz and I were forced to stay low in the turret, which limited our ability to aim the machine guns at the target. The co-axial machine gun was the most suitable option for fighting commandos and infantries in the trenches, not the main cannon.

A loud mix of RPG explosions, machine gun rounds, and bullets tapping against the steel tank made an empty metallic noise. It felt like the gates of Hell were opening. The air was thick with fire and smoke, exploding materials, and dust. The sky and the sun disappeared, and darkness fell upon us.

Boaz was in complete command mode. He directed Tom, the driver, where to move, positioned the turret for Dov, the gunner, to aim and shoot with the co-axial, and operated his machine gun. He did this all at once. I loaded the co-axial machine gun for Dov to fire and stepped up on the loader chair to use my machine gun to add to the firepower.

"Are we crossing over the steel fences?" Tom asked.

"Yes. Go over them. The wires will attach to our tracks, but they won't stop us. We must pass the trenches as soon as possible. We can't stop. Keep an eye on tank number 2 on our right, and don't cross our line of fire," Boaz ordered.

I looked outside as we passed over the first trench. A few Egyptian soldiers fired directly at us, but we couldn't fire back. Our machine guns couldn't aim so low in their direction. I knew that if we stopped, we would be an easy target. As long as we kept moving, they couldn't climb up on our tank.

A few soldiers jumped out of the trenches, terrified by the tanks passing over their heads, panicking as they tried to escape from the tank tracks.

"Tom, you can't stop. Go over them!" Boaz shouted.

The tank started to drive left and right, zigzagging.

"Amir, get a box of grenades, put it on top of the turret, and hand them to me one at a time," Boaz said.

I dived inside the turret, grabbed one box of grenades, placed it on top of the turret, and handed Boaz the first grenade with the safety pin ring pointing in his direction.

I must be careful. With the tank moves and jumps, he could drop the hand grenade inside by mistake.

Boaz took the grenade from me, pulled the safety ring out, counted four seconds, and threw it inside the ditch below the tank.

KABOOM! The loud explosion shook the air.

"I need another one."

I brought Boaz two more grenades and secured them between the loader hatch and the commander hatch so they wouldn't roll back down inside the tank turret. Then I dove back inside to fix the gunner's machine gun and jumped back on the loader chair to fire with my machine gun.

It was like an assembly line, and I acted automatically, efficiently, and without hesitation.

First, I jumped down to load or fix the co-axial machine gun. Then, I took more grenades from storage, stood on the loader chair, and handed them to Boaz. Lastly, I fired my machine gun.

Then it started all over again.

I looked at Boaz. He stood on his chair, exposed from the chest up, took the grenades with both hands from the commander hatch, removed the ring with its safety pin, counted to four, aimed, and threw it inside the trench.

It was the most effective way to deal with the Egyptian infantry in their trenches.

Boaz is a fighter, a brave soldier, and a good commander, I thought.

Tom was driving the tank through the trenches, always passing on top of them perpendicular to their direction to ensure the crossing would be over the ditch, so we wouldn't drop down into it. He chased the enemy soldiers who ran out. Dov turned the turret left and right, looking for Egyptian infantry, and used the co-axial machine gun to shoot them.

The company radio network was busy, too busy. Some tanks had been hit and were asking for support. We broke through the trench lines and started moving toward the buildings. Several Egyptian soldiers came out from the ditches, and the premises, with their hands raised up. Some held white rags, and others threw their weapons to the ground and started running in the desert's direction.

It's over!

We did it.

The Egyptian force has succumbed.

The adrenaline rush I'd experienced started to slow down, my heart stopped pounding so fast, and I had time to wipe the sweat off my face.

We are safe!

A sense of relief washed over me, and my tension began to ease, when a dreadful shriek and a blinding light erupted from the back of the turret. The turret immediately flamed up with black smoke.

I couldn't see anything. I was confused.

Am I injured?

I couldn't see my body, my arms, or my legs.

Am I blind?

My ears were buzzing, and I couldn't hear! I started touching every part of my body. *Nothing is missing.*

I could feel that the tank was moving, and the co-axial machine gun was firing.

Tom is taking us out of the danger zone!

"Boaz, can you hear me?"

Boaz didn't answer.

The heavy smoke slowly dispersed, and I noticed the flames at the back top of the turret, at the communications bay. I immediately took the Halon fire extinguisher and aimed it at the blaze. A jet of gas sprayed over the bay and quickly extinguished the fire. Then I saw Boaz standing on his chair with his legs bleeding.

"Are you okay?" I shouted.

"Yes, I'm fine. What about you?"

"I'm fine too," I said. "The RPG hit us at the back of the turret and damaged the communication systems."

Boaz shouted to Dov, "Tell Tom to follow our platoon commander."

I stood on my chair and held my machine gun, ready to fire. There was no immediate threat. We'd already passed the trenches.

Our platoon commander was driving a few meters in front of us; he'd probably noticed that we had been hit and protected our tank.

Boaz was standing on his chair, fully alert, ready to use his machine gun. He looked at me and said, "We're so lucky."

"You're bleeding from your legs," I said.

"Ah, it's nothing. I don't feel it," he answered. "You're bleeding too, from your arm," Boaz said.

I looked at my arm and saw blood dripping slowly from my elbow. It wasn't painful. Checking further down my arm, I noticed more blood. I opened my top shirt pocket, pulled out my field dressing, wiped the blood, and dressed the wounds. "I don't feel any pain. It's just external," I said to Boaz.

It was quiet. There was still the occasional, random firing of weapon rounds, but the battle was over. Our infantry swarmed the buildings and cleared them of any resistance. A few soldiers rounded an area outside the building with a concertina fence and gathered the POWs there. The Egyptian soldiers sat on the sand in lines, guarded by a few of our soldiers.

Tom followed tank 2, entered the temporary tank parking area, and turned off the engine. We needed to do a lot of maintenance and equipping before going on to our next mission the following day. Loading ammo, fueling, cleaning and oiling the weapon systems, essential repairs, and cutting and removing the barbed wire stuck to the tank's wheels and sprocket with a large wire cutter. All needed to be done.

The technical support team arrived, checked the communications damage, and brought a new radio system as a replacement. Our old radio was burned black. Then the technician connected the other radio and checked each helmet for internal and external transmissions, but they were dead. All the wires inside the turret had been burned out and needed to be replaced.

The company commander's deputy came to check our status.

"This tank won't be ready for tomorrow morning," the technician said.

The deputy looked at us and said, "We have two tents for crew members without tanks at the technical support area. Take your personal belonging and move to the tents. Stay there until you are stationed with new crews."

He looked at me and asked, "Are you the one from the tank that dropped into the canal?"

"Yes," I said.

"Take Daniel's gear, Uzi gun, and sleeping bag, and I'll get you uniform, your size, and other essential stuff," he said.

I packed the items the deputy told me about and went to the tents.

How can I sleep inside Daniel's sleeping bag?

A few soldiers were already there, talking about the fierce combat we had just experienced. They shared information about their friends, the wounded and the fallen, and the tanks damaged during the battle.

I didn't know any of them. They were reserve soldiers, older, and I couldn't see any familiar faces. I wasn't in the mood to talk or share my thoughts and emotions with strangers. I hadn't fully processed the events of that one day, which had started in the early hours.

I found an empty bed with a couple of folded wool blankets, put Daniel's stuff on it, and sat down.

"Guys, look what I found." A soldier, who carried some square cardboard packages in his arms, entered the tent.

Everybody turned to look at him, waiting for him to continue.

He dropped the boxes on one of the beds and said, "It's Egyptian battle rations with goodies. Fava beans, goulash, special crackers, guava juice, and more." He beamed at us.

Wow! What a welcome change after two weeks of eating our IDF standard battle rations.

I sat with the others and tasted the unfamiliar flavors. After a short while, I felt better, more energetic, and less isolated.

I took Daniel's Uzi and walked outside to check on the Egyptian base before it got dark. The few, long buildings, with gravel lanes connecting them, showed evidence of the battle's destructiveness. There were black holes in the walls from shell explosions, bullets marks on the doors, and flames still raged inside some of the rooms.

Outside the center of the base were the air missile posts. Some still stood on their platforms, intact and ready for launch, and some were damaged. Each air missile station was protected by a mound, an earth barrier. I walked toward the posts and climbed the embankment. Broken stations with their missiles pointed to the ground from when the Egyptians had tried desperately to target our troops to stop the attack. A few others had remained undamaged after they'd been deserted.

Dead bodies were lying on the sand, burned and mutilated beyond recognition. What a dreadful sight it was. I stood rooted to the spot and stared at the terrifying scene; it was like watching a frame in a horror movie. Then, I mentally kicked myself out of my stupor and left right away, almost running.

Back in the safety of the tent, I couldn't stop thinking about those dead soldiers. Each of them had a whole life filled with wishes, hopes, and dreams, now doomed by the decisions made by those with more authority, which they probably didn't even have an understanding of or a say in.

War is the gameboard of politicians, in which we, the pawns, have no say.

The sun started to go down, and it got dark. I heard soldiers talking outside the tent and the continuous background noise of generators.

Technical support teams were working nonstop on the damaged tanks, running around the clock to fix and prepare them for the action of the next day.

Then I heard dogs barking and yelping in the distance.

Ah, poor dogs. Maybe they are hungry or thirsty. I should go and check.

I've always had dogs at home since I was a kid. We considered them full members of the family. They gave us loyalty, friendship, and unconditional love, in return for the abundance of food, water, and strokes we supplied them with. The saying that the "dog is a man's best friend" summarized the special emotional connection between me and this species.

I went out of the tent to look for the dogs, worried about their condition, hoping to help. But I never expected to see what was unfolding before me. I was met with a pack of skinny, dirty, mid-size dogs, fighting and growling at each other. They looked like wild animals. I didn't want to get any closer.

A full moon hung low in the sky, partially covered by clouds. Suddenly, the moon came out of the shadows and flooded the ground with a blast of white, bright light. I squinted and focused my eyes on what the dogs were fighting over. I had to step a little closer to be sure it wasn't just my imagination.

The dogs were fighting over a limb! A human body part!

Oh, God! I thought.

What kind of hell is this place, where dogs eat their human friends?

I was shocked and sick to my stomach. Those dead soldiers, though they were my enemy, still deserved respect. They couldn't end up as dog food!

I loaded my Uzi gun, aimed, and stopped…I couldn't shoot. I tried to understand myself, to get my mind straight.

Maybe the dogs are starving, crazed by hunger?

I raised my gun high up in the air and shot once. The dogs were startled and scattered, running until they disappeared into the shadows between the buildings.

CHAPTER 15

Antitank Stronghold, October 20, 1973

"Any drivers here? We have a ready-to-go tank and are missing a driver, is anyone here a driver?" The tent's entrance was flipped open, and I, lying on my bed, saw three soldiers looking at us.

"Guys, we have a tank that was repaired during the night, but we have no driver," the same soldier said.

No one answered. No one was a tank driver.

"I'm a loader," I said, "but we learned how to drive a tank during my tank commander training."

"Great." He looked at me, half smiling. "That is good enough. I'm the tank commander. Pack your stuff and join us in thirty minutes. Your tank is 1A." He turned to leave but stopped and said, "Give me your personal information so I can fill in the paperwork for the next battle assignment."

I wasn't excited to be a tank driver. The driver's cell was at the front bottom of the hull. When the lid was closed, which it was on most occasions, the only view the driver had through his two periscopes was of the terrain directly in front of the tank.

The tank driver's position always reminded me of that of a horse with blinders; he could only see what was in front of him and had no peripheral vision.

As a kid, I had always felt sorry for those horses. I thought it was forced on them as punishment for bad behavior, while the good horses, which were easy to control, weren't made to wear blinders.

On the other hand, being a tank driver was easier and safer than being a commander or loader.

I collected my stuff from the bed and went toward the company. On my way to the tank, I saw the older, tired faces of soldiers who I didn't know. I didn't recognize anyone. The Egyptian base filled up with more tents for technical support and administration. It was organized by the type of support the frontline required.

★★★

I still have time to go to logistics and get some of the stuff I lost. I didn't have any personal items and needed a towel, a toothbrush and paste, a hairbrush, a shaving razor, underwear, clean battle overalls and clothes, a jacket, socks, and a sleeping bag.

I reached a group of tents. One had a big sign reading "Adjutancy," and another, long tent, next to it, was marked "Logistics/Supply."

I entered the logistics tent. "Hello, is anyone here?" I called.

"Be right there," I heard a voice reply from deep inside the tent. A moment later, a soldier came closer and asked, "How can I help you, soldier?"

"I lost everything I had when my tank dived into the Suez Canal. I have only what I'm carrying on me," I said.

"Hmm…I can see you need everything replaced," he said. "Come inside and have a look. Everything is organized in separate piles; some are military supplies, and some are what we got in packages sent to the soldiers on the frontline. Pick a backpack or two and take whatever you need. Sorry I can't help more, but I'm swamped," he said.

Great. That's perfect.

"Thanks," I said and entered inside.

It was a big, long tent. All the necessities were laid out along the bottom of two walls, on blankets spread on the ground.

I found the backpack pile and took two of them. Then I moved to the clothes pile and dug around until I found two sets of medium-sized, clean battle overalls. I went further into the tent, where all the non-military supplies were arranged, and I was amazed at all the stuff I found there. The logistics tent had everything I needed.

A mound of colorful towels, another one of toiletries, khaki woollen socks, and hundreds of pairs of white cotton underwear in a range of sizes.

I filled the backpacks with my wish list, taking only what I needed. Then I went to the sleeping bag area and checked for one that was clean and in good condition. I opened a few and finally chose one that still smelled of laundry detergent.

Next were the coats. I sifted through the stack of jackets, hoping to find the IDF heavy-duty, wintery style, known as "Doobon." But there were only the bulky American types. I grabbed one in my size. From the pile of mess tins and cutlery, I took a set.

My backpacks were almost full to the brim. I looked for two more items which I was still missing, a military water bottle and the standard army belt, which I found, and then went back to the tent entrance.

I didn't find the soldier. "Do I need to sign anything?" I shouted.

"No, and good luck."

Gee, I wonder what "good luck" means in this war?

Is it better to die quickly and end all the misery, horror, and fear? Or maybe return home as a wounded hero, but suffer from your injuries for the rest of your life?

I shouldered the two backpacks and walked to Core Company. Their location was at the south corner of the Egyptian base, just next to my previous company, Braz. I looked around. The only person I knew here was Ami, the tank driver who, like me, had survived falling into the Suez Canal, but I didn't see him.

All the tanks were in their final preparation stages, readying for the moving order to be given. Some soldiers were cleaning the cannons using a special brush, dipped in oil, attached to a six-meter cleaning rod. Others were organizing their stuff in the external storage bins around the tank turrets. Others were just making small talk outside their tanks, ready to jump in when needed.

Braz Company had already started their engines, ready to move. Core Company was to follow them.

I saw my new tank, 1A, and my new crew members.

"Hi, Amir," the commander said. "Organize your stuff inside. We're moving soon. My name is Dan, and as you already know, I'm the tank commander," he said. "Shaul down there is our gunner, and Oz is the loader."

Oz looked at me, "Hey, Amir. Dan told us you're not a tank driver but know how to drive a tank. We can help you if needed," he said.

"That's okay, nothing to worry about," I said. I put my two backpacks, the sleeping bag, and my jacket in one of the external storage bins, then went down and checked the tracks' tension. It was fine. I quickly climbed on top of the steel transmission plates at the back of the tank, opened one, and checked the engine and transmission oil levels. Both were within the acceptable range.

I looked inside the driver's cell, peering through the hatch. Everything seemed in working condition; the transmission gear was positioned on parking, and the brakes were locked. I entered the cell and started the engine. The tank came to life on the first ignition, and I let it run for a few minutes to warm up the engine. Then I climbed out to check the engine and transmission oil levels again. Both measuring sticks showed a mark between the minimum and maximum lines. The tank was ready, and good to go.

I turned to Dan. "Everything looks fine," I said.

"You seem to be a professional driver," Dan said, grinning.

I entered the driver's compartment. It was a confined space. A hard, metal chair with shock absorbers was located below the hatch. I put the Uzi in its allotted spot and sat on the chair. In front of me was a steering wheel and two periscopes. Attached to the floor were large brake and exploration pedals. To my right side, the transmission shift gear with five settings: parking, neutral, low, high, and reverse. The main front panel contained gauges like those of a car: speed, RPM, gas level, engine temperature, battery charge, starter, and more.

I secured and buckled the helmet's straps and connected the communication plug to the tank transmission box. The external helmet frame was designed especially for tank crews and was built from light but durable composite materials. The helmet's interior had two ear pads. A communications box with a microphone arm was on the left side of the helmet and connected to the internal radio via a wire.

I set the chair's height and distance from the steering wheel, the periscopes, and the gas and brake pedals within comfortable reach.

Now, I'm ready.

It was cramped in the driver's cell but secured. The driver sat inside and operated the tank according to the commander's instructions, unlike the exposed loader on the turret, who supported the commander with navigation and enemy contact.

The driver's task was to drive the tank safely and move the crew away from danger. Being a loader required more multi-tasking. A loader had to reckon with weapon systems, ammo distribution, the performance of the machine guns, and firing from his machine gun.

My job now is to look for road obstacles and follow the commander's orders. Much easier.

But, on the other hand, being a driver meant being detached from your surroundings. Visual input was limited; a driver didn't have enough information to gain a thorough understanding of everything that was going on around the tank.

"How do you hear me, and are you ready to move?" Dan asked.

"Driver, sound is clear. I'm ready," I said.

"Gunner, clear and ready."

"Loader, clear and ready."

"We will start moving momentarily. Amir, follow tank 1 and form a battle pattern on his left," the commander said. "Start moving slowly after 1, Amir."

I looked frontwards. A plume of engine smoke and dust obscured my view, but I noticed that the tank in front of me had started moving. I released the brakes, placed the transmission gear in high, and the tank moved slowly.

I followed Dan's instructions of "slower" and "faster," or "a little to the right," or "to the left," among other commands, as the company headed south toward Suez city.

The radio remained quiet most of the time, and nothing much was said except for the few words that Dan communicated to us.

"This is Core Sunray," I suddenly heard on the radio. "In front of us, in about 5,000 meters, there is an Egyptian antitank stronghold. As per our latest information, the Egyptians carry mainly antitank cannons and Sagger missiles. Set your fire positions at 2,000 meters ahead, at the dune hills before us," the platoon commander said. "Platoons One and Three on my right, and Two on my left. Fire at will. Over."

"Our position will be thirty meters from tank 1 on its right side," I heard Dan saying over our internal communications system. "Amir, go ahead. Can you see the old broken drum in front of us? Keep driving in that direction."

I drove the tank, keeping a distance of 100 meters behind and to the right of tank 1, that of our platoon commander, until we arrived at the hillside.

"Go slow," Dan said.

I slowed down.

"Slower now," he said, and I climbed up the dune slowly to turret position until Dan sharply ordered me to stop. I pushed the brakes, and the tank stopped. I knew that Dan and Oz, the loader, were looking for targets.

"Two thousand meters in front of us, antitank cannon," I heard, and noticed the turret starting to turn in the target's direction. Dan continued, "HEAT 2000 enemy cannon," completing the pre-fire command.

I heard Oz loading the cannon. "Loader is ready," he said.

"Gunner is ready," Shaul stated.

"Amir, go ahead a little to hull position."

I released the brakes and slowly drove a few more meters forward.

"Stop," I heard the commander order.

I stopped the tank and put the transmission shift into parking.

Shaul announced, "On target."

"Fire," Dan commanded, and the cannon fired the HEAT shell at the target with a loud blast which shook the tank.

I looked outside through the periscope but could only see the top of the hill. Dust and a smokescreen rose above the horizon.

"Short." I heard Dan say. "Add two."

"I can perform self-adjust," announced Shaul.

"Okay, go for it," Dan said.

The loader loaded the second shell.

Suddenly I heard a loud sound, and the tank swayed and jolted as if struck by a massive hammer. Then it went quiet.

What the hell happened? Was the tank struck by a shell or a missile? But I don't see any smoke or fire inside the turret. I glanced at the gauges. The engine was working just fine. I put the transmission gear in reverse and drove back to a hide position, fully aware that it would interrupt our firing sequence.

Then I heard Dan, "We were hit, we were hit. I'm wounded."

I stopped the tank, put it in parking mode, opened the driver hatch, and got out. I looked at the turret. Dan was bleeding from his forehead. A 10 cm long piece of shrapnel had pierced his helmet at the center of his forehead, just above his eyes.

He stared at me, confused and in shock. Then he took off the helmet with the jutted shrapnel, and I could see the blood dripping.

Immediately, I pulled out Dan's field dressing from his upper pocket, opened it, and held the gauze tight to his forehead to slow down the bleeding.

Oz grabbed the radio microphone and said, "This is 1A. We were hit. I repeat. We were hit. The commander is wounded."

"Stay in the safe zone. I will send you paramedics in a few minutes," answered the company commander.

I looked at the turret. In front of Dan's hatch, there was a massive depression in the tank's thickest and most protected armored section—the front of the turret. An antitank Sabot shell had hit the front of our turret and dug into the heavy steel. Unable to penetrate the armored turret, it had changed its direction upward, spreading steel shrapnel around. One of the bits of shrapnel had hit Dan, who had been standing up, watching Shaul's firing sequence.

Dan wiped the blood from his eyes and looked at his helmet. We all looked at him, stunned, and then at his helmet. I couldn't believe my eyes.

The shrapnel had penetrated the very center of the helmet's protective frame and was stopped by a small, 2-square-centimeter steel buckle inside the frame. Two bands attached by the buckle tightened the helmet around the head. The sharpest point of the shrapnel had twisted the steel buckle's shape, but that small piece of metal had given Dan extra protection. The deadly fragment hadn't been able to penetrate both it and Dan's head.

"This is unbelievable!" I heard Oz murmuring at my side.

Shaul whistled quietly, "Gee, Dan, a few millimeters up or down, right or left, and you'd have been dead!"

The paramedic arrived, took one look at Dan's wound, and said, "God just gave you a gift. The war is over for you. We're taking you to the field hospital." He applied additional dressing to stop the bleeding and helped him into the M3 half-track.

I took the microphone and radioed Core. "This is 1A. The paramedics have arrived and treated Dan. They will evacuate him shortly. We're waiting for your instructions."

"This is Core Sunray. Check if the tank is in operating condition and report," the Core commander ordered.

The tank was wrecked. The mechanical arm system that set the cannon and the co-axial MG's ballistic angle had been knocked out and was now disconnected from the turret.

"We can't use the cannon or the co-axial machine gun," said Shaul.

I called the company commander back and explained the situation.

"Follow the paramedics to the field hospital at the logistic field base and leave the tank in the technical repair depot," he said.

"Wilco over," I answered.

The paramedic settled Dan in the M3 and drove off.

We entered the tank. I opened the driver hatch doors and lifted the driver's chair to better see the terrain. Shaul stood on the tank commander's chair beside Oz, and both guided me on the way as we followed behind the paramedic vehicle.

Driving a tank with an opened hatch gave the driver a better view, but without good dust goggles, it was very tough. Gusts of dust and sand thrown up by the two tracks hit my face and flew directly into my eyes and nostrils. The glasses I had received as a gift from my parents had been left inside the sunken tank. I was using the standard military ones that didn't seal or protect my face properly.

After a few minutes of driving like that, I lowered the driver's seat and closed the hatch lids. My eyes burned and itched, my face was covered with thick soot, and my nose and mouth had filled with dirt and sand.

"Oz, I closed the driver hatch," I said over the intercom. In other words, I meant to say: *Pay extra attention and provide me with more detailed driving directions since my view is limited.*

"Wilco," Oz answered.

I drove the tank slowly behind the paramedics, keeping a safe distance from them, letting my mind drift back to all that had happened in the last couple of days.

These have been the most dreadful two days of my life. I lost two people who embraced me like I was family in the short time we'd been together. When the tank sank into the Suez Canal with Shabtai and Yoav, my heart sank with them.

Then, I joined the second company commander, who treated me kindly but was killed by sudden artillery fire the same dreadful morning. At noon, I fought a fierce battle at the Egyptian anti-air missiles base where my tank was hit by an RPG, the commander was wounded, and the tank was damaged and recalled for repairs. Today, my new tank was hit by an antitank shell, my new commander was injured, and the tank was broken.

"This is freaking weird!" I said to myself, though the words didn't come out.

Is it me? I don't want to sound spiritual, but is it my fate to see the people around me get hurt and killed while I remain unharmed? How on earth do I keep surviving these hellish events? Why me? I don't understand it. I'm not special.

Is there any connection to that odd out-of-body experience I had? Am I protected now?

I was devastated by this highly emotional, roller-coaster ride of thoughts. A heaviness lodged in my chest, and I couldn't breathe.

It's not right that I survive when so many of my friends and the other soldiers around me are killed or wounded. Why me?

Why me?

★★★

After 30 minutes, we arrived at the Ordnance Corps. Oz guided me to the technical service area, then I stopped the tank, turned off the engine, and stepped out.

"What's the problem with the tank?" an officer, who approached us, asked.

The technical repair unit worked day and night and as fast as possible. They wanted to repair every damaged tank as fast as possible, so it could be sent back to its division. Every tank counted on the frontline.

They knew that winning or losing the war depended on their ability to return the tanks to service.

"We took a direct hit to our turret. The gunner said that the ballistic angle compensation system is wobbling, and he can't aim," I answered. "His periscope aims toward the sky without correlating to the cannon position."

The officer jumped inside and, after a few minutes, came back out. "Well, this is a nasty one. The shockwave caused by the shell broke and separated the arm that connects the aiming system to the turret."

"So, what can be done?" I asked.

"It's a complicated repair and can't be done immediately. Even after welding and fixing the system, there is a complex calibration process to be completed. We need to align the cannon with the telescopic sight to get the right ballistic angle for any type of ammunition you might use," the officer said. "Meanwhile, go to the tents on the west side and register with Adjutancy. Tell them your tank won't be ready for a few days so they can assign you to other tanks that need crew members."

I turned to climb back into the tank to grab my stuff when I heard him call after me, "Get all your personal stuff."

We collected our belongings and went to the tents in the direction the officer said. I saw the Adjutancy tent and entered inside.

A sergeant, who sat behind a long wooden table, looked at us and said, "I got a message from technical support that your tank won't be ready for a while. I will take care of you. Here, fill in these forms with your personal information, and then I'll assign you a place to sleep. You can get food in the kitchen tent. Let me know if you need anything else."

We did as he asked, and then he led us to an empty tent with a few field beds covered with wool blankets.

"Stay here until you hear from me," he said before he left.

I put my stuff on the bed, washed my face with water from my water bottle, lay down, and closed my heavy eyelids. My eyes were burning; it felt like sandpaper was scratching my retina. Exhaustion consumed my limbs, and finally I drifted into a deep sleep.

CHAPTER 16

Bad Omen/Outcast,
October 22, 1973

I woke up with a start, drenched in sweat, and looked around. The tent was empty. I was alone.

Hey, what's going on? Where are Shaul and Oz?

The sun was already high in the sky, and inside the tent it was steaming hot. I didn't have a watch. It too had been left in the sunken tank. But even without it, I could guess it was probably around noon.

Oh, gosh, I overslept! Where is my new team?

I got up, feeling famished, and went to look for the kitchen tent. There, I found a few long tables with mounds of battle rations. I opened one package, took the sweetcorn can, drank the juice, and gobbled down the corn. Next on my menu was a can of corned beef. I sliced the meat with the sharp-edged lid and ate it fast in a few mouthfuls, adding a couple of dry biscuits to the mix. I washed it all down with water.

Now, I was satisfied and returned to the tent. Still, there was nobody there. I washed my face, changed into a clean set of clothes, and decided to go to the Adjutancy tent.

The sergeant, the same guy from the previous day, welcomed me with a smile. "Good morning, Amir, or maybe good afternoon. I didn't want to disturb your sleep."

I looked at him in surprise. I wasn't sure if he was being sarcastic or not.

"Where are Shaul and Oz?" I asked. "They're not in the tent, and their stuff is gone."

"Well, they were assigned to another tank in your unit early in the morning," he answered.

"Really? So, what about me?" I asked, annoyed.

"Uhm…I got instructions from the base commander to keep you here." The sergeant paused, scratched his balding head, and said, "You know, Amir, soldiers tend to be less rational in wartime." His tone was hesitant, almost apologetic. Then he continued, "You've gone through a lot in the last couple of days. I heard about everything that happened to you, the tanks, and their crew members. I don't think you need me to remind you…"

He put a hand on my shoulder, looked at me with compassion, and sighed. He was an older man, probably in his early forties, like my father.

"I don't believe in all this bullshit," he said, "but…soldiers are talking and are afraid to take you on as a crew member. Some have even nicknamed you…uhm…I'm sorry…'bad omen.' Maybe rest for a while. Honestly, that wouldn't be such a bad idea." He shook his head and raised his palms up, shrugging.

My jaw dropped, and I stared at him in disbelief for a while. I was confused and speechless.

"What? What do you mean? How was that my fault? I don't bring bad luck to others! I'm not mysteriously protected, no more than anyone else. This is nonsense, pure bullshit," I exploded, offloading my frustration and emotional turmoil onto him. I felt so guilty.

"Hey, hey, relax. No one is blaming you," the sergeant said, trying to appease me, talking to me as if I was a young child. "Listen, Amir." He looked directly into my eyes. "The commanders in your unit reported that you're an excellent soldier, very professional, and brave. This isn't about you, not really! Just a few stressed-out soldiers turned superstitious during wartime."

I couldn't take the conversation any longer. I was so tired and utterly deflated that I turned on my heels and walked away. Back in the tent, I dropped down on the bed and replayed the entire, disturbing conversation in my mind. All my emotions, feelings of guilt, confusion, my questions, and my inability to grasp and understand what had happened, rose to the surface. For the first time, someone had expressed aloud, in clear words, that people thought I possessed extraordinary power over destiny. That I controlled fate for my own protection.

It felt awful to learn that it wasn't only in my head and my heart.

The tent shielded me from the world like a big balloon floating up in the air, detached, giving me a safe haven and isolating me from the harsh reality outside. I was drained of emotion, empty and numb. I was alone, an outcast.

I'm all by myself, and I like it.

Nobody cared to look for me or talk to me, which was fine. I just lay there and closed my eyes. It was hot inside. I flipped the tent walls open, removed my boots, and returned to bed. A light breeze caressed my face, dried my sweat, and cooled me down. I dozed off.

★★★

"Amir, Amir," someone shouted from outside. I turned my head slowly and saw the sergeant.

"The base commander is calling everybody for an urgent meeting and is asking for your presence, too," he said.

"Me? But I don't belong to this unit," I said.

"Yes, but he explicitly told me to bring you in."

"Fine," I answered. I sat on the bed, put my boots on, took my Uzi, and followed the sergeant.

Soldiers were sitting on the ground at the base center, between the field hospital and Logistic tents. Some were standing up, and all were waiting for the commander's announcement.

I tried to blend into the group who were standing. I didn't recognize anyone, there weren't any familiar faces. They looked tired. Even though they weren't frontline soldiers, I knew they worked day and night to provide the troops with what they needed.

The commander arrived, and the chatter went silent. The sergeant had told me that it wasn't a scheduled, routine meeting, and I assumed it must be an important message to put a stop to all of their essential tasks.

"Hello," the base commander said. "I gathered you all here for a few announcements. As we all know, two Egyptian armies invaded the Sinai desert, the Third Army in the south and the Second Army in the north. Our forces crossed the Suez Canal, north of the Bitter Lake, and moved south toward Suez City. Right now, the troops have surrounded the Third Army, cutting their supply of food, water, and ammo, short" he said, pausing to let us absorb his words before going on.

A wave of excitement ran through the soldiers. This was good news, something I hadn't heard for a long time.

"Quiet! Quiet! Let the commander speak," the sergeant shouted.

"This brings me to my announcement," the commander continued when we settled down. "The Egyptians have agreed to negotiate an immediate ceasefire with an American mediator in order to rescue the Third Army from total annihilation."

A loud cheer broke out all around. Soldiers shouted in happiness, "The war will soon be over. The war is over." People laughed and smiled broadly, patted each other on the shoulders, hugged, and shook hands.

"Please, guys, settle down. I am not done yet. I have more issues to talk about." The commander's voice was raised.

We immediately fell silent.

"The war is not over yet. We all must remain fully vigilant. Under the current circumstances, both armies will expand their attacks in a last-minute attempt to gain better terrain. We received intelligence that tonight, the Egyptian forces will try to get control of a tactical area five kilometers south of our base." The commander stopped and looked at us from one end of the crowd to the other. "Only tomorrow morning, the Americans will map the areas under our control and the Egyptians'." He paused again, and the soldiers around me nodded, watching him gravely.

I thought the commander had finished with the announcements, but then he held his hand up to stop us from leaving and said, "The next item I have to talk to you about is not as positive."

All paid full attention.

"One of our field service units is in a desperate situation," the commander said. "We got a service request from one of Gir's tanks with an engine problem. The tank was stuck in a valley about five kilometers south of here. The company evacuated the crew and continued toward Suez City. The tank was left behind for us to repair."

"We sent one of our mechanical repair teams to the tank two hours ago and got a message that the tank is beyond on-site repairs. They decided to leave it to be towed later, and return to the base. Unfortunately…" he paused and sighed heavily, "when they started driving back, they were attacked by a barrage of bullets and RPGs from the cliff just above them. Their half-track was struck immediately, but they managed to escape unharmed and ran back to shelter under the rock. Now, they're trapped there," he said in a hushed voice.

"I believe that after Gir Company left the area, the Egyptian commando came over to expand their lines before the ceasefire. Now they are waiting until sunset to kill our team and destroy the damaged tank."

Silence descended, thick and heavy. This was hard news to take in.

"So, what are we going to do? They are not frontline fighters or combat soldiers. The Egyptians will slaughter them!" one of the soldiers called out.

And another added, "Yes, and we have only four more hours until sunset."

"Yes, we know the urgency of the situation, and the risks," the commander said. "That's why I asked you to gather here. I'm looking for volunteers who can drive a tank."

I heard a few whispers, and then silence. No one stepped forward to volunteer. The base commander turned his head in my direction, spotted me, and asked bluntly, "Amir, can you drive a tank or be a tank commander?"

I was surprised he knew my name. Everybody turned to look at me as if they all knew who I was. That was an extremely unpleasant and stressful moment; one could have heard a pin drop. I glanced around and met their eyes as they waited for my response.

Why are they staring at me?

I couldn't read the soldiers' expressions. Fear. Anxiety. Blame. Sorrow. Challenge.

"Yes," I answered. Something inside me compelled me to agree.

"Do you want to volunteer? We must try and save them," the commander asked again.

"Yes," I said.

"The meeting is over, guys," the commander said. "Go back to your work."

People gathered in small groups, murmuring and whispering to each other, and then left the area.

"Amir," the commander approached me. "We need to talk about the plans to rescue the team. I thought you could use your damaged tank and drive quickly to their location, gather them all inside the turret, and drive back. The tank will protect you all from bullets. Let's go to my tent and discuss details." He turned and led the way.

I followed him, not saying a word. Thoughts swarmed through my mind like a colony of wasps.

I don't care that he asked me to do the mission. I'm not afraid. No! And I don't care about bullets, or RPGs, or the antitank missiles that Egyptian commandos carry. I hope I will do a better job saving them, than I did with my friends!

I shrugged my shoulders, slightly.

We entered the commander's big tent, and he placed a large, colored, Sirius code map on a long desk. Then he took a black marker and circled an area on the map. He glanced in my direction to check I was paying attention and said, "This is our base location."

I followed his index finger as he pointed to another spot on the map. "And this is where our technical team is trapped with their half-track." He marked a black X on that point, which was about 5 kilometers south of our base.

I looked at the map and saw that the terrain around our camp was flat until it reached the wadi where the X was marked. It was located under a tall, steep cliff alongside the wadi edge.

The commander took a red marker and marked another X, overlapping the first black one. "The information we received shows that the Egyptian commandos are here." He pointed at the red X.

I looked at the red mark. It was about one hundred meters from the mechanical team's location. The commandos were situated just above them, on the cliff.

Oh…the Egyptians are right on top of them.

"What a fucked up situation!" I murmured as my brain started to evaluate my options. "I will be fully exposed to the commandos' fire until I can get underneath the rock, where they can't aim at us. And I'll also be exposed on my way back. If I want to navigate between their fire, I need a driver. Otherwise, it will be a useless, deadly mission," I said to the commander.

I felt the adrenaline coursing through my body as I talked to the commander. I didn't feel any fear. Not one bit.

How come I'm not afraid? Do I believe in this stupidity, that nothing bad will happen to me, that I'm protected? What nonsense! But what if it's real?

"Okay," he answered. "I will find you a driver."

"And...I'll need to see the area myself before I go, to find reference points on the flat terrain to guide me to our soldiers without using the map."

"That's a good idea," the commander said. He picked up his field phone receiver, and said, "Bring me my Jeep now."

A couple of minutes later, I heard the Jeep coming to a stop in front of the tent. I grabbed the map and went to the vehicle. The commander drove south, and I traced our way on the map. After a few hundred meters, he stopped, and I stepped out and marked up on the map a few empty oil drums that I'd noticed. We continued south about two more kilometers from the base, and the commander stopped again.

"We are getting too close. Do you want my binoculars?"

I took the binoculars and looked south. I saw a burned tank between us and the location of the trapped technical team. It was an excellent visual object to mark on the map. I looked at the map again, trying to find another item that would be able to guide me to the team's location, when I saw the high, white cliff above the flat terrain, and the wadi in front of it. Even without binoculars, I could easily see the Egyptian commandos' location at the top of the cliff, above the place where our trapped soldiers took shelter. The distance from the burned tank to the commands was 1–1.5 kilometers.

"Any thoughts, Amir?" asked the commander.

"Yes," I said. "This is the plan. We will drive as fast as possible to the burned tank, from there, to the team's location, take them inside the tank and escape as quickly as possible. The driver must drive at high-speed and in a zigzag pattern, so it will be harder for the commandos to lock their missiles or other firearms in on our tank. It will be a very bumpy ride."

"Okay, sounds like a plan," the commander said in a low voice. He stared forward, his expression grave and thoughtful. "Look, Amir," he suddenly said as he turned to look at me. "I have two options: the first is going with your rescue plan in the hope it will work out, and you all come back safe and...alive...The second is to cancel it, and then..."

He didn't finish voicing his thoughts and looked down, but the meaning was obvious. The Egyptian commandos would kill his technical team, but he would spare the lives of myself and the tank driver.

"No, we can't leave them there!" he suddenly raised his head and called out in frustration. "We must try to save them, Amir. Don't you think so?"

I felt that he was pleading with me for understanding, for approval. It felt like he was making the hardest decision ever, gambling with the lives of the soldiers under his charge.

"Yes, I do," I said. "IDF does not leave soldiers behind enemy lines." That was the ideology I'd grown up with. We were "The People's Army" and, as such, we were responsible for each other.

CHAPTER 17

Rescue, October 22, 1973

We drove back in silence. When we arrived, a soldier was waiting for us in front of the commander's tent. The commander stopped the jeep and said, "Amir, this is Ron. He will drive the tank."

I looked at Ron. "Are you a tank driver?"

The soldier gazed hard at me as his lips set in a tight line. "I'm not a tank driver," he said curtly. "I'm a professional mechanic, but I know how to move a tank. And I'm not a combat soldier," he added hurriedly.

"Fine. As long as you know how to move it and can follow my orders, that's good enough," I said.

The commander listened to our conversation. "Our radio frequency is Bravo 56.75, and the tech team is using the same frequency. I will be tuned in for the entire duration of the mission. Don't forget to report your progress to us. Is there anything else I can help you with?" the base commander asked.

"No," I said, "I'll pick up the tank right away." Then I turned to Ron. "Let's go to the repair depot and find my tank. We must leave now."

The tank hadn't moved since I brought it there. I climbed into the turret and stood on the commander's chair. I lowered it so only my head and shoulders would be out of the hatch and put the lid at 45 degrees for extra protection. I put on the loader helmet, connected it to the commander communications box, and set the frequency to the Bravo channel. Holding the commander control stick in my hand, I turned the cannon to 3 o'clock to make the driver hatch more accessible in an emergency evacuation. *Anyway, I can't use the cannon.*

Ron entered the driver's seat, connected his helmet, and tested the tank's internal communications. He sounded clear.

"Ron, close the hatch and let's go," I said.

"Bravo, this is Amir. Can you hear me?" I checked our radio signal with the base.

"This is Bravo Sunray. You sound clear," the commander replied.

"I'm leaving now. I will give status updates when we reach the burned tank and on arrival at the technical team. Over," I radioed.

"Wilco," the commander said.

"Let's go," I ordered.

Ron started the engine, and we were on our way.

"Turn left," I guided Ron, and the tank started to turn. "Now go straight." The tank stopped turning and started to drive straight ahead, to the south.

"Good. Now, go faster," I said.

I looked at the terrain in front of me. It had a hard, flat surface covered with small pebbles, which meant the tank could advance fast. But I needed some time to explain the plan to Ron step by step, so he would be clear about what I expected of him, and what he needed to do.

"Ron, we're heading south toward a burned tank. It's about one-and-a-half kilometers from here. Soon, you'll see it. At that point, the white cliff which our technical team is trapped below will become visible, but at that point the Egyptians will be able to see us and will start shooting." I paused for a moment to let him take in the information.

"This means, Ron, that we will be exposed to their fire from the burned tank until we reach the team. What I need you to do, from the moment they start shooting is to drive fast in a zigzag pattern. On my command, every five to ten seconds, you'll change the tank direction. That will minimize the chance of us taking a direct hit. We have about two kilometers to reach the team, less than a fifteen minute ride. So drive fast and zigzag. Is that clear, Ron?" I asked.

"Okay...I...understand," Ron answered.

I could hear the hesitation and anxiety in his voice.

Well, it's natural that he's afraid. After all, he doesn't have battle experience. Strangely enough, I wasn't frightened. Not at all.

My damaged tank couldn't fire or fight and, in its current condition, served only as an armored vehicle. The only way to survive the mission was by using three tactics: surprise, speed, and constantly changing our direction. It was vital that we completed the task as quickly as possible.

"Ron, drive slowly until we reach the burned tank. We need to minimize the dust and smoke we're creating so we can take them by surprise."

We passed the oil drums at a slower speed. At this point, we were about 2.5 kilometers from the cliff.

"Ron, the burned tank is straight ahead now. Can you see it?" I asked.

"No, I can't," he answered.

"Look through the periscopes."

"Yes, yes, now I see," Ron replied.

"Continue slowly until they start firing at us. No reason to attract their attention any sooner than necessary." I began to feel the stress building up.

We got closer to the burned tank, and I radioed Bravo. "Bravo, this is Amir. We're now passing the burned tank."

"This is Bravo, good luck," the commander replied.

The ground in front of the tank started to tremble. Dozens of rounds hit the earth and raised clouds of sand and dust. A few missiles whistled past the tank and exploded nearby, and the sky was lit up by multiple shrieking tracer bullets. A blend of cacophonous noises.

I ducked inside the turret, only the top of my head exposed. I peered out of the hatch, and watched the scene taking place around us.

"Faster! Go faster!" I shouted to Ron.

Ron pushed the gas pedal down to the floor, and the tank roared as it accelerated.

"Turn right."

Two seconds later, I said, "Now, go straight for ten seconds."

"Turn left."

Then, "Go straight."

"Ron," I shouted, "continue in a zigzag, full gas, and I will give you corrections."

The tank moved wildly, turning left and right, again and again.

I've lost the cliff. I can't see it. I must get higher above the hatch; otherwise, we'll miss it.

I raised my body out of the hatch up to my chest and saw the precipice on our left.

"Ron, go left," I said.

Ron turned the tank.

"Now straight."

Ron corrected, and the tank faced the rock.

"Now zigzag in this direction, full speed," I said and lowered my head again. *Phew! Everything will be fine as long as I can see the cliff and the tank moves quickly in its direction.*

The escarpment became larger and larger.

"Ron, keep going. A few hundred meters, and we're there," I said.

Now we were very close us. RPGs exploded, and the earth around us bubbled up like oil boiling in a frying pan. Bullets hit the tank armor, and the sky above was still illuminated with the red tracer bullets.

The firing suddenly stopped. I raised my head a little and saw that we were directly under the rock edge.

"Slow down! Slow down immediately," I shouted.

The tank reduced speed, and I directed Ron to stand alongside the other damaged tank. He stopped the engine. Suddenly there was silent. We were out of the Egyptian force's firing line.

I climbed down the turret. "We did it, Ron," I said as he came out of the driver's cell.

He didn't answer or even look at me.

The five technical soldiers came out from behind the other tank and looked at me with obvious appreciation and excitement. A few of them hugged me, patted my back, and shook my hand.

I was emotionless.

"Hurry up, guys, enter the tank. We must leave now," I said and noticed Ron was the first to climb up the turret and get in.

What the fuck is he doing?

"Hey, Ron, where are you going?" I asked him.

"I'm done with driving. I'm not driving the fucking tank anymore!" he yelled back.

The other soldiers entered the turret after Ron and squeezed inside. It was very crowded, and I wondered if it was even possible for six people to stand in there.

It's good that the cannon is positioned in the three o'clock direction because, that way, the team has more space in the turret and more room above the driver cell.

I went up the turret. My seat, the commander's, was taken by one of the soldiers. "Can anyone drive the tank?" I asked.

No one replied. Some, though, shook their heads.

Great! Now what? The only way we can escape from this hellhole is if I drive the tank. I'll have to lift the seat and stick my head out of the driver's cell so I can see as much as possible.

Then to my surprise, the technical soldiers in the turret closed and sealed the two hatches with the steel lids. I guess they thought it was safer that way.

I entered the driver's seat and put my helmet on. I had no connection to Bravo, and could only reach the internal intercoms system, to which no one inside the turret was connected anyway. I shouted up to the turret, "We're leaving now. Hold tight. It's going to be a bumpy ride."

They called back, "We're ready."

I started the engine, disconnected the brakes, and put the tank into a high gear. We began to move.

The Egyptians are probably waiting for us, ready to fire. I should use the same tactics as before, and drive quickly in a zigzag pattern, I thought. There wasn't going to be anyone to help me with suggestions or directions. But since we were going to be moving away from the cliff, I would be protected by the turret, though my head would be fully exposed.

Ugh…I have no eye protection. This might be a problem!

I pushed the gas pedal all the way down, and we moved forward, leaving a big cloud of smoke behind us. Then, at full gas, I turned the tank roughly in the direction of the burned tank. From the driver's position, I couldn't see it. I zigzagged violently, counting three seconds turning left, then going straight for ten seconds, then three seconds to the right, back to straight drive for ten seconds, and repeated the pattern.

As long as I keep counting the seconds, the tank will head north. But I must change up the pattern; otherwise, the enemy will anticipate my moves.

I heard the technical team in the turret struggling to keep balance. Someone complained, but the others shushed him immediately and told him to shut up. My eyes started to burn, and I instinctively squinted to minimize the effect of the dust and sand blowing into my eyes. But I couldn't drive without seeing the terrain. I shook my head.

Maybe I should lower the chair and look through the periscopes. But that wasn't an option as no one in the turret could guide me without an internal communication system.

BANG! BANG!

Bullets began to hit the turret, and RPGs or missiles, I couldn't tell which, exploded nearby. I continued with my wild zigzagging and didn't hear any more sounds, other than from the team inside with every strong turn I took.

So far, so good! But where is that burned fucking tank? I should have seen it by now!

I turned to the right, and finally, the burned tank appeared; it was about 400 meters away. I turned toward it.

God, I'm so lucky. Now I just need to find the oil drums, and then, we're out of danger. Phew…probably about two more minutes until we reach the tank. We were close, and I continued to zigzag, trying not to lose sight of it.

My eyes were on fire. I took the water bottle and splashed water on my face, but it didn't help. Now my face and eyes were caked with wet sand and mud.

I could see that the tank was very close and decided to pass it on my right side. *Now, I need to look for the drums, my next landmark.*

Suddenly, the tank shook violently.

What happened? Are we hit? I don't see any smoke, and the engine sounds okay.

Intense screaming and hysterical shrieking came from the turret. I looked back in the turret direction and noticed it had shifted from the 3 o'clock position to the 6 o'clock.

"Is anyone hurt?" I shouted to the team as I continued driving.

"We're fine. The turret swung all of a sudden, and we were surprised. Ron's screaming, but I don't see any injuries. We're still checking him," someone said.

I couldn't understand what had happened to the turret or why it had moved. Then it clicked. Most likely, I came too close to the burned tank on my right, and our cannon, positioned in that direction, must have hit it and turned automatically thanks to the sliding safety fixture.

I continued driving rapidly, zigzagging my way to the drums. Now I could see them clearly. *And once we've passed the drums, we will be out of the Egyptians' firing range.*

Then I can slow down.

A few minutes later, we were back at the logistics base. I brought the tank to a stop in the center of the base, locked the brakes, and turned the engine off. I climbed out of the driver's cell and walked directly toward my tent. I didn't want to see or talk to anyone.

A few of the people from the mechanical team followed me and blocked my way.

"Hey, man, thank you," one said and excitedly grabbed my arm.

"You saved our lives," another shouted.

"Yes, we owe you our lives," somebody else pitched in.

Clapping their hands, they shouted, "You are our hero!"

I tried to shrug my shoulders, to distance myself from their overly emotional reaction. I wasn't comfortable. "What happened to Ron?" I asked, trying to change the subject.

"Nothing happened. He just had a panic attack. Physically, he's not hurt," one of them answered.

Then the base commander arrived. "Amir, you did a great job. Thank you," he said with a broad smile and patted me on the shoulder.

I didn't respond. I glanced at them all and said, "I'm going to my tent." Then I turned and left. I could hear them cheering, shouting, talking loudly, telling the commander about the ride back, and laughing. I didn't feel anything. The ONE thing I wanted was to be alone.

★★★

I arrived at my empty tent, washed my face, removed my boots, and washed my feet. It had gone dark outside. I went to the kitchen to grab some cans and returned to my tent.

Around 10:00 p.m., I heard loud explosions and saw lights coming from the south, and then the sergeant suddenly entered the tent.

"Hi Amir, how are you?" he asked.

"I'm fine," I said.

"We're celebrating the successful rescue operation. You saved the lives of the mechanical repair team, and the commander wants you to come and celebrate with us." He looked at me with anticipation. "You've performed exceptionally," he added when I didn't answer.

"Thank you, Sergeant, but I'm exhausted. I'd prefer to stay here and have a good night's sleep."

"Sure, I can understand that. I will let them know."

"What were all those explosions?" I asked.

"Ah, those. The Egyptians destroyed the tank and the half-track that the team left behind. As I told you before, you saved their lives. If you had not brought them back, they would all be dead by now."

CHAPTER 18

Ceasefire, October 24, 1973

"Amir, I've been looking for you," said the sergeant. "I hope you got some rest yesterday. Your battalion called, and they need you back urgently. They want to assign you to a tank. Our brigade is missing many tank crew members after yesterday's disaster," he said with a grim expression.

"What happened?" I asked, alarmed.

"Yesterday, our brigade, together with a few infantry units, tried to capture Suez City before the Americans enforced the second ceasefire. One of our battalions was tasked with attacking the city from the north. The town seemed deserted until they reached its center. The Egyptian forces ambushed them; they were hiding in the top floors of the buildings there and fired down into the narrow streets. They used everything in their arsenal. You name it," he said, and started counting off a list of weapons on his fingers. "Grenades, RPGs, machine guns, and AK-47s.

We suffered many casualties, especially from the tank commanders and loaders who were standing up at the turrets." The sergeant paused, shook his head in disbelief a few times, and sighed.

"Our progress was completely halted. The line of tanks were trapped in the tight alleys, and many were destroyed, the wreckage blocking movement on any direction of the streets. The infantry was lost in the side streets, and it took our forces hours to disengage from the city and evacuate," the sergeant said. He looked visibly distraught.

I could envision the hopeless situation our units had gone through.

The narrow streets at the city center must have forced them to ride in a tight convoy line, one after another without intervals. The Egyptian ambush would have hit the first and last tanks, causing the rest of them to stop in their tracks, unable to escape the fire from above. The tanks in the middle of the line might have tried moving to the side streets, hitting the buildings as they went, which probably brought them crashing down over them.

Tanks were useless for this kind of battle. Cannons and machine guns couldn't aim or shoot at the tops of buildings. The maximum height angle for a cannon or a co-axial was about 28 degrees. Also, the loader and commander's machine guns were attached to the turret with a fixture that limited their firing angle.

I could imagine the crew's devastation and their desperate attempts to return fire with their Uzi guns, standing exposed on the turrets. I sensed their frustration at their inability to use any of the tank weapon systems, which would have left them no option but to sit inside behind closed lids.

★★★

The sergeant continued. "Anyway, the task for today is getting ready to move the field hospital closer to the frontline, and then the repair service depot, too. But for now, I need to drive you to your battalion. Collect your stuff, and I'll be back in five minutes with the Jeep," he said.

We drove south on a black, paved road alongside the Sweet Water Canal. After a short ride, we arrived at the brigade base.

He stopped the Jeep at the Adjutancy tent and turned to me. "Amir, this is it. It has been a real pleasure meeting you, and, uhm…good luck. Don't hesitate to ask if you ever need anything I can help you with. We…are all in your debt for what you did for us," he said, and offered me a handshake.

His voice was thick with emotion, and I shook his hand and nodded.

I took my stuff, threw my bag over my shoulder, and turned to him. "Thanks," I murmured. I felt indifferent about what I had done that day. I didn't feel anyone owed me anything. The sergeant's gratitude and emotion made me uneasy. I didn't deserve it, I felt. "Good luck to you, too," I said.

The sergeant waved to me and drove away.

★★★

"Amir? We're waiting for you," I heard a flat voice, coming from inside the Adjutancy tent, say.

I walked inside and saw a middle-aged first sergeant major. His shoulders were slumped, and his eyelids were heavy, half-closed. He looked stressed, grave.

"There is a tank crew who are missing a commander. We will give you a ride there and assign you as their tank commander," he said. "The tank is 3B, and the company name is Braz."

I raised my eyebrows. "I have been part of that company before," I said.

He looked me in the eye. "I know," he said. "The ceasefire is now in effect. Be aware of snipers in the northern part of the city. They're positioned on high-rise buildings; you can't see them, but from time to time, they try to shoot in our direction. The distance from them to your tank is about one kilometer, so it's out of their effective fire range, but..." he raised his hand in the air and shrugged. "Don't put yourself or your crew at risk. Stay low on city side. Also, you must not return fire without a direct order from your company commander. Any questions before we leave?" the first sergeant major asked.

"No," I answered.

"Okay, then. The command car is outside, and I'll drop you off at your tank location. It's only a couple of minutes' drive. But first, I have two short stops to deliver food supply to the other tanks. Your tank will be the third stop."

He was very efficient. Two cardboard food boxes were already on the back seat, one for each tank. The delivery process went quickly and smoothly as he radioed the tanks ahead of time so that they'd be expecting his arrival.

"Now we are going to your tank," he told me.

The tank was parked away from the others. The company had spread itself thinly to cover a large area. It was quiet and peaceful. There were no shrieking bullets or RPG explosions to be heard. No foul air thick with smoke from explosions and burned oil. No shouts about direct hits or injuries over the radio. Nothing. There was no evidence of the traumatic events that had occurred only a few hours earlier.

The parking area looked like a small piece of heaven on earth. On the left side of the tank—the east side—there was a two-meter height dike, to prevent flooding from the Fresh Water Canal. The water traveled from the south to the north at a slow, tranquil pace. Along the shallow banks grew beautiful, dense cattail plants, the same plant that my mom and I used to collect back home when I was a kid.

My mother would put them in a tall, elegant, crystal vase and place them in our living room. Our friends and neighbors often warned her that one day, the cattails would bloom and fill our house with white, cottony masses of tiny seeds. But my mother had always shrugged off this fearmongering, which, after all, had never materialized.

A little further down the river, I noticed a loud flock of wild ducks swimming and quacking in the canal and, from time to time, diving into the water in search of food. Tall palm trees and dense, green vegetation covered the shores with abundance.

From the south, I saw the road to Suez City; the high-rise buildings in the northern part of the city looked quiet and non-threatening. Beyond the city's limits, the view turned to the sickening yellow vistas of the desert.

The command car stopped behind the tank.

"Here it is. This is your tank," the first sergeant major said.

The main gun was directed southwards toward the city's buildings, and I noticed a slight movement. *Probably the gunner searching for threats through the periscope.*

A head appeared from the loader hatch. "Hey, Benjamin, did you bring us a tank commander?" the soldier asked.

"Yes, Mike," the first sergeant major answered. "Come down. I brought you your food supply."

"What delicacies are on today's menu?" Mike asked.

I smiled at that same, daily joke.

"Today, and just for you, there's a big surprise. We have…uhm…a box of…battle rations," Benjamin answered, fully collaborating with the joke, probably for the ten-thousandth time.

Mike came down from the northerly side of the tank, careful not to make himself the target of a sniper's cross, and Benjamin handed him the box.

I got out of the command car, bringing my stuff with me, and introduced myself to Mike.

Benjamin waved us goodbye, started the car, and drove away.

"Hi, guys," I said to the other two crew members. "Can you all come out?"

They climbed down from the rear side of the tank and approached me.

"Hi, again. I'm Amir, your tank commander. Our mission is to watch this area, guard it, and protect ourselves from potential threats. As I was informed, there are snipers in the city's high-rises, but we are out of their firing range here. However, we will still take extra precautions, and any outside activity will be done at the north side of the tank, the rear, to keep us protected."

The three soldiers looked at me attentively and nodded their heads.

"We'll keep one of us on guard at all times, day and night. The schedule will be split between the four of us, and guard duty will take place in the loader hatch, using the binoculars to watch over the buildings and the area surrounding them. If you spot a threat, use the loader machine gun. And, finally, remember that the ceasefire is now in effect on both sides," I said and paused. "Any questions or updates?" I asked when no one reacted.

"No, Amir. Everything is clear. This is what we did before, but now the load will be divided between the four of us rather than three. It'll be much easier," Mike answered.

I organized shifts and set the first, mine, from 7:00 p.m. to 10:00 p.m., and my second shift twelve hours later, at 7:00 a.m. to 10:00 a.m. the next morning.

The night was quiet except for the sounds of the nature surrounding us; like the hums of the small waves in the canal that broke against the earthen dams and then ebbed away. The light breeze that whistled softly between the cattail plants, and the rustling of the palm trees. All of which were very relaxing, and lulled me to sleep.

There's nothing to be alarmed by, I thought.

Quack. Quack. Quack. A loud flock of ducks dived into the canal and woke me up at sunrise. It was probably around 6:00 a.m. I stretched in my sleeping bag and yawned.

Ahh…what a perfect way to wake up.

Soon after, my morning shift started.

The radio suddenly started breaking up as I was changing guards at 10:00 a.m. "3B, this is Braz Sunray. Do you hear me?"

I took the microphone and answered, "This is 3B. Loud and clear. Over."

"Is this 3B Sunray?" Braz Sunray asked.

"Yes, this is 3B Sunray," I said.

"Shabtai's father is heading to you in a jeep. He wants to talk to you since you were the last person to see him alive. Over," he said.

I stopped breathing as a jumble of thoughts raced through my mind, one after another.

Oh, God. What am I going to tell him? His son is dead, and I'm alive! Shabtai had had the best chance of survival; he was the one who warned the rest of us! Why didn't he jump out? It didn't make any sense then, and it still doesn't now!

Why am I alive?

I felt so guilty to have survived.

★★★

"Wilco," I said automatically.

Every tiny detail of what happened surfaced in my memory and played like a slow-motion movie, from the moment when Shabtai had shouted, "*Jump out of the tank*," to that bleak reality when I stood on the west-side canal bank, calling their names again and again. Not giving up hope of hearing their voices in response to my own, and of finding out they had survived.

What am I going to tell him? Your son is dead because he didn't jump. He saved my life with his warning and he could save himself if he had jumped. We both were at the same location on the tank turret…

Why didn't you jump, Shabtai? Why?

And what if his father thinks I should have done more to save his son?

But I couldn't do anything for Shabtai! He should have jumped out of the tank like I did. Instead, he entered into the turret. Why? Why did he do that?

I needed to understand. It wasn't logical, the way Shabtai had reacted. I stared out of the turret as my mind tried to deal with that enigma.

Maybe Yoav had a problem getting out of his cell, and Shabtai tried to pull him out? I heard Yoav screaming at Shabtai, first asking for his help and then yelling at him to get out of his way.

★★★

I saw a jeep coming toward us with two high-ranking officers; it stopped next to the tank, and I climbed down the turret. I approached the vehicle and looked at Shabtai's father. *His name is David*, I remembered. *Just like my dad's.*

"You are David, Shabtai's father," I said.

He looked somewhat surprised. "Yes. How do you know?"

"We met once before when you visited Shabtai," I said.

"Ah, I see," he said. "Can you tell me what happened? I understand you were the last to see him. I can't get any more information from anyone else."

What the hell! None of the brigade and battalion commanders have dared to tell him anything! They've left it to me to tell him the horrible news of his son drowning in the canal? How can I do it? What can I possibly say to a father who has lost his son?

I felt sick to my stomach and decided to detail the event the way I'd experienced it and remembered it.

"On the eighteenth of October, late at night, we arrived at the crossing point. The ferry had already loaded the last tank from the previous company, which had crossed before us. We were the first tank in our company to pass the canal."

Shabtai's dad stood stiff and tall and listened carefully. His face looked taut and grim as he tried to take in all the information.

"The Egyptian artillery," I continued, "shelled us constantly, so I entered inside the turret and fell asleep on the loader's chair. At one point, I woke up and noticed we were moving back to the east bank. I asked Shabtai what was happening, and he told me we were having some mechanical problems and were going back to wait for another ferry."

Shabtai's father didn't move his gaze from me, entirely focused on my words.

"I entered the turret again. Shabtai was awake, alert, and standing on his commander chair. Suddenly I heard him shouting, '*Wake up! Wake up! We're tipping over. Prepare to jump.*'"

I closed my eyes briefly, hearing Shabtai's voice in my mind. When I opened my eyes, David was staring at me without blinking. His face looked ashen.

"I pushed myself out of the turret, crouched against the lid, and prepared to jump when the time was right. In a minute or so, Shabtai called out again, '*Jump from the tank.*' The tank started sliding slowly toward the rail at the lefthand side of the ferry. I looked for Shabtai but couldn't see him. He entered the turret, and I heard Yoav yelling, '*Help me out! Let me out.*'" I paused again. The whole scenario was still so vivid; it was playing itself out in my mind.

I licked my dry lips and went on. "We had no time. The tank started tipping over. I removed all the heavy stuff I had on me, and when I thought the tank had tilted about forty-five degrees, I jumped as far as possible," I said.

"Why didn't he jump?" Shabtai's father asked in a hollow voice.

"I don't know. Maybe he thought Yoav needed help to get out, and he tried to pull him out."

"Was that the last time you saw him?" David asked.

I nodded in reply.

"After the *Zodiac* pulled me out of the water, I asked about other survivors. They told me that, to the best of their knowledge, only two crew members had been rescued from both tanks. I asked them to go back and search again, and they did, but they didn't find any other survivors. The *Zodiac* dropped me on the west bank of the canal. It was almost dawn. I stood in front of the water and looked for any sign of movement. I was expecting them both to emerge out of the dark water. I couldn't understand why Shabtai didn't jump. But I didn't see anything. Then I started calling their names, shouting them over and over, until the *Zodiac* operator told me to shut up so as not to draw the Egyptians' attention."

I stopped talking and looked at David.

He stood on the spot, immobile, his face pale and blank, emotionless, and I thought maybe he didn't understand what I was telling him.

Shabtai's and Yoav's faces were clear in my mind, and a deep sense of grief gripped my heart until I couldn't breathe.

In my mind's eye, I saw them inside the dropping tank, holding tight. And when the water rushed in, I saw them losing their orientation and struggling desperately to find the hatch in the darkness of the deep water, fighting for their lives.

I didn't just leave you there, Shabtai, Yoav. I tried to find you. I called your names and prayed you would find your way out from the tank under the water and swim to the surface. I explained this to them silently.

"I didn't want to leave them there," I said to Shabtai's dad in a hushed voice. "I thought it wasn't over yet. I couldn't just leave, so I stood on the bank and shouted to the water just like that..." I cupped my hands around my mouth and shouted, 'Shabtai...Yoav...Shabtai...Yoav...' until the *Zodiac* team silenced me."

David looked at me, not saying a word, and then turned back and told his driver, "Drive back to the battalion's headquarters."

They left without a backward glance.

CHAPTER 19

Ceremony, October 26, 1973

"To all Braz stations, this is Braz Sunray. Prepare your crew and be ready to move in ten minutes. Acknowledge receiving my message. Over," I heard the radio blare.

Tank by tank acknowledged receiving the order.

"Place everything inside the external storage bins and enter your cells," I instructed my crew. "Everything left behind will be lost, as I don't know if we'll be returning to this location. Be ready in ten minutes."

Ten minutes later, our company commander started to move out. All tanks followed him in order. As tank 3B, we were the last in our company, after 3A. I entered the convoy, leaving enough space in front of us to avoid accidents.

The company moved north. After a few minutes, I saw our battalion tanks were parking in a long line facing west. The company commander ordered us to join the line in the same order that we'd travelled in. When we finished, all three companies formed a straight row. The infantry and other support forces were positioned on both ends of the line. We were all aligned and waiting.

Then, I heard the radio instructing us to change the frequency to the battalion's channel.

"This is your battalion commander. Today, I can say that we've successfully accomplished our mission. We have saved our nation from destruction. And though we still have a long way to go, we can all be proud of our achievements. You all played a most important part in reaching this moment," the commander said in a celebratory tone. But when he continued with his message, his voice lowered.

"But we can never forget the many sacrifices we have had to make in order to win this bitter war. Our friends gave their lives for our nation and for us, and I want all of us to salute them the way they deserve," he said. "Turn your main guns at maximum elevation and load HPDS shells. Be ready to fire on my command."

Thirty tanks loaded their main guns with HPDS shells.

The battalion commander said, "Commanders and loaders, stand on your chairs and salute our heroes. They gave up everything and will never return home," he said.

All the battalion tank commanders and loaders raised their right hands in salute.

"Fire," the battalion commander ordered, and 30 tanks fired together, the loud blasting shaking the ground.

"Last but not least," the commander started saying when the loud sounds of the shooting had subsided, "before we go back to our daily assignments, I want all the cadets from the Academy for Tank Commanders, who joined us and fought side-by-side with us, to step forward to my tank."

I climbed down the turret and walked toward the battalion commander's tank, the first tank in the procession. Five more soldiers followed me. I didn't recognize any of them.

The commander waited for us, standing tall, and when we reached him, he said, "Please, stand in one line. Attention!"

We formed a straight line and stood at attention.

"Commanders!" he said. "Today, you're getting your sergeant rank. Now, you're officially tank commanders. Congratulations!" He gave us a crisp salute.

That was very surprising news. We all saluted back, but one of the cadets said, "But we didn't complete our training."

"Each cadet who served with us during the war is more than qualified for his new rank and capable of acting as a tank commander," the battalion commander answered.

He lifted a yellow manila envelope from the ground, opened it, and pulled out the three-stripes military ranks. Then, he stepped between us and attached the stripes to our sleeves with safety pins. "It is my honor to give you your new military ranks. I know that it's only a matter of formality for some of you, as you've already been assigned as tank commanders. Thank you for your service. May God be with you, and let this be the last war. Commanders!" He saluted us again.

THE END
BUT NEVER FORGOTTEN

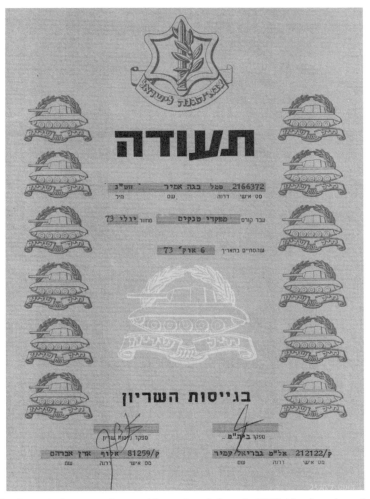

The author's Tank Commander certificate dated Oct. 6, 1973 (the first day of the Yom Kippur War) and signed by Avraham Adan, Major-General.

Appendix

Shot-Kal shells. From left to right: APDS (Armor Piercing Discarding Sabot)—Qty 30; HEAT (Shaped Charge round)—Qty 12; HESH round (High Explosive Squash Head)—Qty 30. (Wikimedia)

Shot-Kal cannon ammunition (1973)	HESH	HEAT	APDS
Caliber	105 mm	105 mm	105 mm
Round mass (nominal)	20.5 kg	22.1 kg	14.5 kg
Round length	938 mm	992 mm	838 mm
Muzzle velocity at 21°C (nominal)	731 m/s	1,173 m/s	1,539 m/s
Maximum range	9,510 m	8,200 m	16,739 m

★★★

Letter to Shabtai's father that the author wrote immediately after the war. It was added to Shabtai's memorial booklet.

לדוד היקר רב שלומות!

להשלמת הרקע לעלון לזכר בנך, הנה הספור בו היה מפקדי במשך שמונה ימים ולילות ארוכים מאד, אשר קשה לעלותם בכתב.

9.10.73 — יום חמישה

היום לאחר יום לחימה נתקענו בעמדת אש כאשר הנע ימין הלך. טנק שכן חילץ אותנו והגענו לכביש באיזור "הברנה". לא הספקנו לנוח רגע והנה מופיע טנק פגע וממוריד טערקשן והמט'יק השחור מפיח ואבק שואל אם יש טערקשר. מיד עליתי לטנק אשר הפחיד בתחילה. מראה אדם חרב אשר היה בתאי, והצוות החדש אשר אנשי מהם לא הכרתי הזווה משבר אשר עובד על חיל העובר מטנק לטנק. שבתאי שאל לשמי וניסה להכניס אותי לאוירה הנוחה שהיתה בצוות זה. שבתאי לא חיכה דקה נוספת, הפלונה היתה זקוקה לעזרה והוא רץ קדימה אפילו ללא חימוש של טנק. ההתקפה היתה רצינית והפלונה עמדה בעמדות בלי־ מה, כאשר בכלים לא נותרו אלא מעט פגזים, אולם קולו השקט של שבתאי נתן הרגשת בטחון בצות למרות שאני יודעתי שנותרו 3 פגזים אחרונים. לקראת ערב נשברח ההתקפה וחזרנו לחניון לילה. למרות שחיינו עייפים עבדתי במרץ רב, יודעתי שהפעם זכיתי במפקד טוב.

10.10.73 — למחרת — קמנו בבוקר השכם, תפסנו עמרות והתחלנו לירות לכיוון ההסתערות של המצרים. השמדנו מספר טנקים, איני זוכר כמת, אולם הצלבים שעל מזן התתחן הלכו והתרבו (יואב היה עושה צלב על כל טונק שהדליק). לעת ערב חזרנו וחימשנו והתכוננו למחרת.

11.10.73 — כרגיל כמו שיגרה השכמה, תפיסת עמדות וקרב בלימה, אולם הפעם לשם שינוי שבי וכך היה:
שבתאי זיהה חיל מצרי קט'יק מרחק רב והודיע לבמבה (כוח סיור), אולם במבה לא נעה לאיסוף החיל. שבתאי לא היסס ונסענו לכיוונו. השבוי נשכב על הארץ ושבתאי ללא פחד קפץ מהטנק, בדק אותו לקח את אקדחו תעלה אותו על הטנק ונונו לו לשתות מיד. חזרנו לכוח ומסרנו את השבוי לבמבה ושבתאי החזיק באקדח.
בשלב זה כבר הכרתי טוב את אנשי הצוות והדבר הוסיף לאוירה הטובה שהיתה בטנק.

12.10.73 — שום דבר מיוחד קצת מנוחה שבתאי מארגן את הפלונה בהיותו סמ"פ מוסר דוחות, מארגן צוותים מחלק ציוד ומתפעל את אנשי החימוש לתיקונים בטנקים בעיקר בעיות קשר.

Continued

14.10.73 — עד שעה 9.30 יום מנוחה. לפתע, באמצע החימוש הודעה על תנועה. נסענו במהירות וכאשר הגענו ל־ "הברגה" נדהמנו לראות כיצד טנקי טירן ישראלים נסוגים ובעמדות מצוידים כלים בוערים. תפסנו את העמדות בדקה ה־90 כאשר טנקי האויב כבר בעיצומה של ההסתערות טווחים של 500 מ'. שבתאי תפס ב־ פינה מבודדת עמדה כאשר לפתע זיהה 5 טנקים עולים עלינו. שבתאי בשלווה האופיינית לו נתן לתותחן פקודת אש אולם המטרה הוחטאה. ה־3 כבר היו קרובים מאוד, ירינו שוב והם שינו כיוון ונסוגו, אחר כך השמדנו עוד 2 טנקים שנוספו לרשימת. שבתאי זיהה רכב רך — מכונית אזרחית מעה לכיווננו ודיווח ל־ מפקדו. התשובה היתה להשמידה. הכנסתי חלול וה־ תותחן ירה, הפגז חלף בס"מ ספורים מעל גגו של ה־ רכב ולשמחתנו הרבה המכונית הושמדה ע"י טנק אחר. משום מה חיתה לצוות הרגשה לא טובה לירות על רכב אזרחי ובפעם הראשונה שמחנו שהחטאנו.

15.10.73 — יום מנוחה — יפה ירקוני מופיעה לפני האוגדה והחיילים כבר מנחשים כי משחר, יותר מקרבות בלימה מתכונן לנחות עלינו. ואכן בשעות הערב אוסף מפקד האוגדה את החילים והמפקדים ומודיע על הכוונה לחצות את התעלה לקראת בוקר. שבתאי מיד בא ונתן הוראה לכל החילים לגרז את חטנקים לקראת החציה ואנו מחכים לפקודת היציאה. למחרת עדיין מחכים בהמתנה, עושים רחצה ראשונה (עם ניריקנים), חופפים ראשים ומסבנים את הפנים (מורידים כמה שכבות פיח) ולפתע מתגלים פנים חדשות של אנשים ולא מסכות שחורות.

17.10.73 — היום מקבלים פקודת תנועה חשבנו כי הכוונה היא לחציה, אולם מגיעים לאיזור האגם המר. שטח מישורי ללא עמדות ואדמת פודרה לבנה המעלה ענני אבק להמוניהם. אנו עומדים בשטח מישורי, אין ע"מ מדות, אין מסתרות ואין אויב, לפתע ללא כל אזהרה מוקדמת נורה טיל לכיווננו, שבתאי נותן הוראה לנהג להסיע את חטנק, כל שניה יקרה. "אחורה ידית שמאל ידית ימין" ונחלצנו. הטיל פגע בטנק שכן.

אנו מנסים לטהר את השטח באש נק"ל אולם המקלעים לא עובדים עקב האבק הרב. לאחר טיפול פרוק תשמון הם מתננים שוב ואנו מרסטים את השטח מרחוק אנו מזהים מספר טנקים בוערים. זכר למארב הגדול שהיה. לעת ערב חוזרים חזרה ונתקלים במארב רציני. החשיכה המוחלטת נדלקת באלפי כדורי נותבים, טילים ופגזי נ"ט הנגורים עלינו, שבתאי מורה לכבות כל תאורה בטנק ולהמשיך, השירה ממשיכה כאשר החשיכה מחווה מסתור באיסיות מחוץ למארב בו עולים מספר טנקים על מוקשים. המהומה גדולה

Continued

המ"פ נפצע ושבתאי תופס ללא היסוס את מקומו.
הוא יוצא מהמיצר נוסע כ-2 ק"מ חחוצה ומתחיל
לאסוף את הפלוגה וחהגדוד המפוזרים ברדיוס של
קילומטרים. בתחילה יורים זיקוקים באויר ושהם
אוזלים מתחילים לירות נותבים לזיהוי מקומנו. לאט
לאט מתקבצים הטנקים סביבנו. שבתאי מארגן אותם
לפי פלוגות וההתנועה נמשכת בחשיכה המוחלטת.
מאוחר בלילה הגענו לחניון ושבתאי מארגן את הפלר־
גה ומצווה צווחים, מניעים מחדש מחמשים ומתדלקים

18.10.73 — הגיע הבוקר, הגדוד מתארגן לחציית התעלה,
נוסעים בצד חכביש כאשר שבתאי מוביל את הפלוגה.
שאלתי אותו, מדוע לקחת על עצמך תפקיד זה והתשר־
בה היתה : הרי מישהו חייב לעשות זאת. בדרך היתה
התקפת מטוסים ומינים ירדו על שירת הדרגים בכביש.
איזור החציה היה אפוף עשן אפור, לאט לאט קרבנו
לאזור החציה ונכנסנו לחצר. חיכינו זמן רב משום
שתנועת החציה התעכבה עקב הארטילריה הממושכת
שירדה באיזור. לאחר מכן לקראת הערב חתחדשה.
אנו היינו הראשונים בפלוגה לחציה. עלינו על הדוברה
וטנק נוסף עלה בעקבתנו. הדוברה החלה לנוע לגדה
המערבית של התעלה שלפתע הבחנתי שמשהו לא
כשורה, הדוברה לא הצליחה להגיע למקום עניגתה
בצד השני, לאחר כמה נסיונות נפל לתקן בעיה זאת
ניסו להגיע לגדה המזרחית אולם דבר זה לא עלה
בידיהם. חית שקט ואני צפיתי בחציה. לאט לאט
שקעתי בשינה שלפתע התעוררתי ושמעתי את שבתאי
צועק : לקפוץ מיד חחוצה. שבתאי הבחין כי הדוברה
עומדת להתהפך יצעק לצוות לחלץ עצמו והוא עצמו
לא קפץ אלא העיר את התותחן וניסח כגראה למשכו
החוצה. הטנק גלש למים כאשר הרגשתי את המים
עזבתי את הטנק ומיד שקעתי במערבולת הגדולה
ולאחר שניות מספר עליתי שוב על המים. הלילה
חיה שחור משחור, פה ושם שחו חיילי הנדסה ונאספו
ע"י סיירת גומי. עליתי על הסירה ושאלתי מי מה־
צוות נמצא. מכל שני הצוותים היו שניים בלבד אני
והנהג. יואב ושבתאי והצוות של הטנק השני לא היו.
הסירה עשתה מספר סיבובים ולא מצאה חיילים ב־
מים, צעקתי וקראתי בשמותיהם, אולם תשובה לא
באה. הגענו לחוף לחציה הפצרתי באחראי על הסירה לעשות
סיבוב נוסף ועליתי על טנק מ"פ פלוגה ר'.

מרגע שהכרתי את שבתאי ז"ל למדתי מחו מפקד טוב
נאמן ומסור לחייליו. למרות שעברתי מפקדים רבים במלחמה
קשה להשוות את יכולתו, אומץ ליבו, מסירותו וטוב־ליבו
למישהו אחר.
הוא היה מפקד מעולה ובראדם טוב.

אמיר בגה — סערקשר.

The following is a translation of the original letter in the photos above.

Dear David,

Here are the events of the long, harrowing eight days and nights in which Shabtai, your son, was my commander.

Oct. 9, 1973—Meeting:
After a long day of combat, my tank was hit, and we were stuck, exposed to enemy fire without the ability to move. Another tank towed us back to the safety of 'Havraga' area. Shortly after, without a moment of repose, another tank appeared. It had taken a hit, and one of the crew was taken away on a stretcher.

The commander, dirty and blackened by soot and dust, asked if any of us was a loader. I confirmed that I was and climbed up into his tank. The blood spattered inside my new cell was disheartening, and meeting the new team, a group of strangers, didn't add to my confidence. But these were not unusual emotions for those who changed tanks in the middle of a battle.

Shabtai asked for my name and tried to make me feel at ease. Soon after, he took off without wasting another moment. The company needed help, and he didn't even wait to arm the tank with more ammunition.

The battle was hard, and we fought the attackers with little ammunition. Shabtai's quiet voice instilled a sense of security in me, even though I knew we had only three shells left in our arsenal. In the evening, the attack broke down, and we returned to the makeshift camp for the night. There, despite our tiredness, we worked together to prepare our tank for the next day of battle. I knew then that this time I had got a good commander.

Oct. 10, 1973—
The next day, we reached our positions early in the morning and fought long and hard to defend our line from the Egyptian tanks. We destroyed many tanks. I don't remember the exact number, but the marks on top of the gunner's shield were plenty. Yoav, our gunner, used to mark an

X for every tank he took down. We returned to our campsite in the evening and prepared our tanks for the next day.

Oct. 11, 1973—
Another day of fighting and defensive battles as before, but this time with a twist—a prisoner of war.

Shabtai noticed an Egyptian soldier, an officer, walking toward us. He informed Bamba, our Scout Unit, but they weren't interested in picking up an enemy officer. Shabtai, without hesitation, ordered our driver to approach the Egyptian. The officer lay on the ground, and Shabtai jumped down from the tank and approached him without fear. He talked to him in Arabic as he checked his uniform for weapons, and took a handgun he found in his possession. Then he told him to go up into the tank, seated him, and gave him a canteen of water to drink from. We returned to our post and transferred the POW to Bamba. Shabtai kept the handgun.

At that point, I had gotten to know my team members, which added to the good atmosphere we had in our tank.

Oct. 12, 1973—
A rest day. There were no battles to command or lead, yet Shabtai was very busy. As the deputy commander of our company, he organized our workload, wrote military reports, checked our ammunition, and ordered replacements and repairs from the technical unit.

Oct. 14, 1973—
At 9:30 a.m., still working on loading the tank up with ammunition, we were ordered to move immediately to our location on the battlefield. When we reached the Havraga area, we were shocked to see the Israeli *Tiran* tanks had backed away from their positions, leaving behind a few burning Tirans.

We had arrived at our location at the very last minute, when the enemy tanks were already within short range, about 500 meters. Shabtai set us up in one corner of the area when suddenly he noticed five tanks moving toward us. In his quiet tone, he ordered Yoav, the gunner, to open fire. Yoav's first shot missed. Three tanks were getting very close. We shot again, and the three tanks turned back and retreated. We destroyed the other two tanks, which Yoav added to his list.

Shabtai then spotted a soft target—a civilian car driving in our direction. He informed his commander and got an order to destroy the target. He gave the order to Yoav, who missed it by mere inches. Another tank fired and hit the car. Somehow, we all felt it wasn't right to fire at a civilian target. For the first time, we were happy to have missed.

Oct. 15, 1973—
A rest day. In the evening we had a music show.

There was a change in the division. Whispers and quiet conversations between the soldiers anticipated a shift in the direction the war was taking. That evening, after the entertainment, the division commander announced that we would cross the Suez Canal the next morning.

Shabtai gave the orders for the company to prepare the tanks for the crossing. We waited all night and all morning for the moving orders. In the meantime, most soldiers got a chance to wash their faces and hair with jerrycans of water. Suddenly, we discovered that we all had new faces—cleansed of soot and shaven of ten days' worth of stubble!

Oct. 17, 1973—
On this day, the moving order was given. We thought we would be crossing the canal but reached the Great Bitter Lake area instead. The land there was flat, without anywhere suitable for or anywhere to hide, and covered with white, powdery dust that travelled high into the air. There were no military postings, no enemies, no targets.

Suddenly, out of nowhere, we heard and then observed a rocket flying in our direction. Shabtai immediately instructed Ami, the driver, to drive back, right, and left, and we were out of range. The tank next to us was hit.

We tried to use our machine guns, but they had been jammed by the sandy soil and weren't working. After a quick clean and some oiling, they 'sang' again, and we sprayed the area with bullets. From afar, we saw burning tanks, a vivid reminder of the ambush we had encountered earlier. On our way to the campsite, we were ambushed again. That was a much more difficult confrontation. The dark night sky was lit up with thousands of tracers, rockets, and antitank shells, all aimed at attacking us. Shabtai ordered us to turn off all lights in the tank, and the convoy moved slowly out of the ambush. A few tanks rode over landmines, and a big mess ensued.

The company commander was hit, and Shabtai, his deputy, now assumed the position of commander. He led us out of danger with brilliant tactical maneuvers. After a ride of about two kilometers, he began gathering the rest of our company and the battalion, who were spread over a distance of many kilometers. We began shooting tracers and firecrackers to help them locate us until slowly, very slowly, the remaining tanks gathered around us.

Shabtai organized them into companies, and we continued on our way back to the camp in complete darkness. We arrived late at night, and Shabtai reorganized the companies and crews and ordered us to prepare the tanks with gas and ammunition so as to be ready to move out early in the morning.

Oct. 18, 1973—
Morning. The battalion was getting ready to cross the Suez Canal. Shabtai led the company over the dunes, parallel to the road. I asked him, "Why did you take the position of company commander?"

"Well, somebody had to do it," he gave me his answer straightforwardly.

Egyptian MiGs attacked the ordnance unit which had been riding along the paved road. I saw black smoke, but the convoy continued onwards. We slowly approached the crossing point; it was under continuous attack by heavy artillery. The whole area was covered by clouds of gray smoke. The crossing was delayed, and we were told to stay back and wait for our turn. By early evening, the process was started again.

Our tank was the first to climb on the flatboat, followed by another. The ferry started moving toward the west bank of the canal. But I noticed something was wrong—the ferry couldn't reach the dock. After several unsuccessful attempts to fix the problem, the ferry turned back toward the east side but couldn't move.

It was quiet, and I watched the other ferries sailing from one bank to another until I fell into a deep slumber. Suddenly, I heard Shabtai shouting, "Jump out immediately!"

Shabtai had noticed that the ferry was about to flip over into the water. He called his team to jump out of the tank and save themselves. He didn't jump himself, but went to wake the gunner and probably to help him out of his chair.

The tank slid into the canal, and when I felt the water, I jumped off the tank. I was immediately pulled down into a strong vortex caused by the massive weight of the sinking tank. After a moment, I swam up to the surface.

The night was pitch black. A few soldiers from the Engineer Corps swam near me and were pulled up onto an inflatable boat. I climbed up onto the boat and asked who else had made it. Only two members of the two tanks that had sunk into the canal had been rescued—the tank driver and me.

Yoav and Shabtai, along with the team from the other tank, weren't there.

The dinghy circled the area a few times, but no more soldiers were discovered in the water. I shouted and called their names, but didn't receive any answer.

When we reached the bank, I pleaded with the soldier in charge of the boat to do another search for Shabtai and Yoav. I was then ordered to join the tank of Company F's commander.

From the moment I met Shabtai, I sensed what a good commander he was, always responsible and devoted to his soldiers. I have served under a few commanders in this war, but they make no comparison to Shabtai's resourcefulness, bravery, dedication to his missions, and kindness.

He was an excellent commander and an exceptional human being.

Amir Bega—Loader.

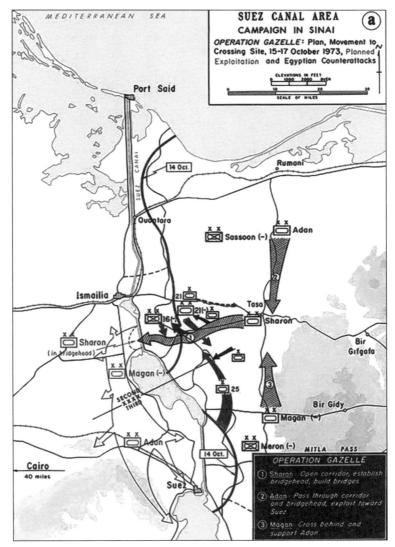

Map documenting the crossing of the Suez Canal. (U. S. Military Academy)